HAPPINESS CAME WITH A CAT

My journey from brokenness to happiness, and the life-lessons my cat taught me.

CYNTHIA STAR

"Cynthia's adventures with her cat are an inspirational romp on the road to self-discovery. You'll love being along for the ride as they learn from each other and distill big spiritual lessons into simple truths."
–Jessika Aalbregt

NEW EDITION

Published by Cynthia Star Books Publishing

www.cynthiastarbooks.com

Copyright © 2023 by Cynthia Star

All rights reserved. This book or any portion thereof may not be reproduced or used in any manner whatsoever without the express written permission of the publisher except for the use of brief quotations in a book review.

Contact: Facebook/CynthiaStarBooks.com@cynthiastarbooks

ISBN: 979-8-9850681-5-3

Cover Design

Rob Bockholdt

PREFACE

This copy is a revision of my original book. The story is the same, but I added more details, giving my readers more of what they asked for.

To the reviewers that were disappointed because I skimmed over painful details, unwilling to share the deep stuff, I apologize. You were right; I wrote the original as feel-good synopsis of what happened, leaving out much of my suffering. If you read the first version, I hope you will give this book another chance and a fresh review.

To members of my family that were an integral part of getting me through my darkest days, I regret not adding you to my first story. If I hurt or disappointed you, I hope you will forgive me. Hopefully, I did you justice this time.

EDITORIAL REVIEW

Happiness Came With a Cat is a journey.

Not only does the book go over the author's journey, but getting it to this stage has been a journey in and of itself.

The first time I chose to read this book, I was intrigued by the title – for obvious reasons. I enjoyed the book, but it felt like it was missing something – a certain level of depth that the author was hesitating to dive into.

Upon learning that her book might be able to help other people in her situation if she let her readers in, Cynthia went back to writing, again, and again.

Cynthia had to go back to the darkest times of her life for this book, and relive them to write them as articulately as possible, and her efforts paid off.

This version of the story is deep, real, raw, detailed, relatable, and inspiring, all while still being a quick, fun, upbeat read with a sense of humor – basically, all things one hopes to find in books of the genre.

~Fatima Aladdin
I have a master's degree in English Language and Literature

"Happiness is always on the other side of fear."
~ Margie Johnson

DEDICATION

To the people that loved me along the way.

Thank you to my mother, Betty Jean, for her unconditional love, to my daughter, Brandie, for her tender care, and to my brother, Jeff, for giving me hope. To Calli Rae for teaching me to be a better Mom and to Grayson for always being there.

A special thank you to my good friends, Lisa and Leslie for their selfless acts of kindness and to Margie for sharing her wisdom, strength and love along the way.

To my wonderful friends that tucked me under their wings. I mentioned some of you by name in this version, but for those I didn't, thank you for your part in my healing: Amy, Ann, Carla, Claudia & Karina, Erin, Katie & Larry, Jim, Jocko, Kay, Lee Ann, Matt, Rod, Roger, and Sally.

TABLE OF CONTENTS

PREFACE	3
EDITORIAL REVIEW	4
DEDICATION	6
INTRODUCTION	9

LESSON #1:
CATS ARE BETTER THAN PEOPLE   15

LESSON #2:
SOMETIMES HATE TURNS INTO LOVE   27

LESSON #3:
CHANGE IS PART OF LIFE   35

LESSON #4:
WE ARE NOT IN CONTROL (ESPECIALLY WITH CATS)   59

LESSON #5:
HOME IS WHERE YOU FEEL LOVED   71

LESSON #6:

ATTITUDE OF GRATITUDE EQUALS A HAPPY LIFE   87

LESSON #7:

WHAT YOU FOCUS ON EXPANDS   97

LESSON #8:

CATS ARE AN EXCELLENT JUDGE OF CHARACTER   109

LESSON #9:

HAPPY IS AS HAPPY DOES   135

LESSON #10:

TWO ARE BETTER THAN ONE   145

LESSON #11:

CATS ARE SMARTER THAN PEOPLE   159

EPILOGUE   165

ABOUT THE AUTHOR   169

INTRODUCTION

The first time I saw Mr. Jinx, he did not impress me. He had scraggly hair that was full of dandruff and matted in places. His tail had bare patches where he'd pulled the hair out, and he acted stressed. We were at the animal shelter, in the cat playroom, getting to know the cats offered for adoption. He had been there a while, and it soon became apparent why. He was bad-tempered and hissed at the other cats if they got too close. Watching him puff up to twice the size, I envisioned that long hair clinging to furniture inhabiting every corner of my house, and I was not the least bit interested. But my daughter fell in love. She didn't seem to mind that he bit and scratched her as she rubbed his belly or that he looked like an alley cat. But I did.

I liked the big gray and white beauty rubbing against my leg. She had short, soft hair and resembled Hobbs, the precious feline we lost.

"This is the one, Calli. I like this one," I told my daughter. The gray and white cat was perfect as far as I was concerned. She was mellow with age, friendly, and had short hair.

She ignored me, playing with the scraggly-looking cat.

"Oh Mom, this one is so cute."

"I don't want a long-haired cat, Calli. I don't like him."

"But look at him, Mom, he's the best one here," she said, pleading with me.

"Please Mom, I want this one," she said, holding his furry face next to hers and giving me her most convincing smile.

"No Calli, I told you. No long-haired cats."

We visited the shelter after months of debate with my new husband. He refused to let me get another cat after Hobbs passed. My kids and I had her for fourteen years before we got married. She grew up with them, and we all loved her. We had a dog; he reasoned. One pet was enough.

It wasn't like I was asking to have multiple cats, just one cat to fill the space of the one we lost. But he kept saying "no cat" every time I brought up the subject. I knew getting a cat might cause trouble. But my youngest daughter, at seventeen, didn't just want a cat. She NEEDED a cat. She was distant, rebellious, and getting into trouble at school. The cat offered companionship and to heal past hurts. I felt the power of this cat, touching her heart and imploring me to take the chance.

I stood there, debating about which cat to get and wondering if I was brave enough to face the shitstorm it was going to cause. The words of my best friend's husband entered my head.

"Tell me why you can't have a cat. Isn't it your house? Don't you pay at least half the bills? Didn't you have a cat when you met him?" If my girlfriend had spoken the words, I might not have listened. She had to support me as a woman and my friend. But the haunting words didn't come from her. They came from her husband, so for me, they held more validity.

He was right, of course. There wasn't a good reason we shouldn't have a cat. I had a cat when he met me. I only wanted a cat to replace the one we lost. The one my kids and I grieved. I didn't know the decision I made that day would affect my life so much.

My daughter and I spent the rest of the afternoon shopping for cat paraphernalia. We got a new litter box, a big cat tree, toys, food, and, of course, a brush designed for long-haired cats. She promised to groom and care for the cat she had begged to have.

The shelter required twenty-four hours before we could take Jinx home. They needed time to check us out and decide if we were responsible cat owners, and it gave us time to consider the responsibility of pet ownership. My daughter and I were ready, but my new husband wasn't.

The cat stuff was in the kitchen when he got home. My husband looked around and said, "We're getting a cat?"

"Yeah," I said, "He's so cool! Wait until you meet him."

Without a word, he spent the next three hours packing his stuff. I didn't stop him or try to talk him out of leaving but started cleaning the house, acting as though things were fine. Inside, I was dying. Frantic, afraid, grasping for anything to stop this, but I knew it would have been like trying to stop a freight train going a hundred miles an hour. I remained silent, watching as he loaded his pickup, placed his wedding band on the counter, and drove away.

That sounds crazy, right? But that's how things in our house had become. He had extreme reactions to the smallest things. Like when I took him out for his birthday, and the waitress mentioned it, even though I gave strict instructions NOT to say anything to the person taking the reservation. The poor server realized her mistake too late. We exchanged icy stares. I had done the unforgivable, and the evening was ruined. I regretted it immediately. He didn't like to be the center of attention, but I thought if I made it clear to the restaurant not to say a word, they would honor my request.

The only reason I mentioned it at all was they were famous for their complimentary birthday dessert, and my husband loved dessert. He wouldn't talk to me the rest of the night or for weeks to come. I walked home; he drove off. Walking the mile home felt better than being punished with silence. What was supposed to be a celebratory date turned into another reason for him to be angry. His birthday card remained unopened, tucked in the visor of his truck for the next 6 months.

I picked Jinx's name from a childhood cartoon. My daughter and I both thought the name fit the scraggly cat with the long hair. He later earned the title of "Mr. Jinx" as he became the king of the house, but I'm jumping ahead.

When I brought Jinx home the next day, I didn't know he was going to become my life coach and that together; we had embarked on a long journey of self-discovery, healing, and happiness.

LESSON #1:
CATS ARE BETTER THAN PEOPLE

My first lesson from Jinx proved to be the most painful. I adopted the cat, and my husband left. His leaving extended much deeper than me bringing home a cat. The need for control? He's the man, and what he says goes? I disobeyed, and he was making me pay? Oh, I paid.

Everything was fine, or so I told myself. I wasn't responsible for my husband's behavior or what he did. The only person I could control was myself and my reactions, so on the surface, I was fine. But below, in the depths of my soul, a powerful force took over my body. Some people may label it grief, mourning, or loss. I never found a medical or psychological explanation for what I experienced, despite searching for years and Googling such phenomena. Perhaps someone out there knows the answer to this mystery, but I never figured it out. My conclusion is that you can die of a broken heart.

Missing someone so much that you can't eat or sleep. That was me. I longed to hear his voice, the weight of his steps in the hall, the rise and fall of his chest when he slept. The way he'd say he loved me. Grief consumed me like a lion devouring my flesh.

As usual, I continued to work. I attended counseling and church, sought comfort from my friends, cried, grieved, and thought I handled the loss well. My counselor told me to let my husband sit in his own stuff and let him come to me, so I never tried to call him.

I would drive around our little town, searching for his truck with my heart pounding, tears filling my eyes, not sure what I would do if I found it, but wanting to know if he was still around. My heart felt like a cake cut into two pieces. Only half remained in my chest, the other half wrenched out. Every time the phone rang, my heart jumped, hoping it was him. I must have checked it a hundred times a day. The sound of a passing vehicle, a knock on the door, or the ding of a new text was always a possibility that it might be him. But it never was.

I assumed that he rented a place if he remained in town. I never found his vehicle parked in a strange driveway, but one day I spotted the red Toyota where he worked. Relief washed over me, knowing he was still in town. Seeing his truck filled me with hope and a sense of relief. I drove away without contacting him, even though I wanted desperately to see him, to fix things, to go back to the way we were. Even if it was dysfunctional, it seemed better than this torture. But I kept my distance and applied what my counselor said, waiting for him to make the first move.

The stress and pain of my husband leaving cast me into a darkness I have never known. I became the main character of Stephen King's book, Thinner, where a curse placed upon the protagonist causes him to lose weight no matter what he eats. It was fun at first. Yay! I can eat whatever I want and still lose weight. But I had little extra weight to start with, and I continued downhill. My body began eating itself from the inside out, and I was powerless to stop it. I slipped from 110 pounds to 105 to 99, 98... clear down to 93 lbs. I was a walking skeleton with a gaunt face and protruding bones. I continued to lose weight despite consuming up to five thousand calories a day. It was terrifying to watch the lifeblood drain out of me, one pound at a time.

My oldest daughter, Brandie, came home for a couple of weeks to care for me. She made all my favorite foods, adding extra fat and calories to each recipe. The daughter I had once nursed and spoon-fed was now my caretaker, trying to mother me back to health. She introduced me to protein shakes, enticed me with fat-laden treats, and encouraged me daily. Although I didn't gain any weight, I didn't lose any, either. Her presence was calming, her smile infectious, and I'm certain she saved my life.

I always wondered if this strange phenomenon of my body starving itself was associated with my eating disorder from earlier years. For thirteen years (age thirteen to twenty-six), I binged, purged, and starved myself. At its height, my disorder controlled everything in my life as though it was a second person inside my body that took over.

That's another book in the making, but for now, it's merely speculation that my body resorted to starving itself like an out-of-control memory permanently ingrained in my psyche. The difference is when I had the eating disorder, I purposely purged or starved to lose weight. This time I ate non-stop, yet could not gain any weight. Interesting paradox, isn't it? Whatever it was, I was powerless to stop it.

Jinx arrived, and my husband left. I spent long winter nights alone. That darn cat. I knew it wasn't the cat's fault, but he was the antagonist in my story. Everything inside me wanted to blame him. If we hadn't adopted him, my husband would still be here. Jinx was the character I wanted to hate.

A well-written villain is more than just a bad guy. They have qualities you can't help but like. On some level, you relate to them because you see yourself in them. They do bad things for good reasons or good things for bad reasons. Some villains do bad things for bad reasons. Those are the worst, the ones you hate. But Jinx had a good side. He made my daughter happy, gave her a reason to smile, and helped her deal with her emotions. He snuggled with her at night, greeted her at the door, and cooed to her in cat tongue. The two of them had their own language, carrying on entire conversations that I never understood. He also brought a sense of normalcy. We had Fat Cat for 14 years before she passed; having a cat again made our house feel like home. He was here, and my husband left. Damn husband.

After three months without a word, my husband called and wanted to talk. I remember the day he called. I stared at my phone as it rang... his name lit up across the screen. Frozen, I let it ring. When I picked up, his voice was calm. My heart raced, my mouth went dry, and tears filled my eyes as he asked if we could meet.

"Of course. Where?" I asked. "Today? Sure. Our favorite spot?"

We sat in his truck, parked by the lake, the sun beaming in the windows. He later confessed that when he first saw me, he thought I might die. He hadn't seen me in over three months, so my emaciated body was a shock.

Imagine my surprise to find out he wasn't in an apartment or a house. He had been living in his truck during a Wyoming winter. What?

He expressed anger at me for not calling, leaving him alone in the bitter cold. Like it was my fault you chose not to get a place? It was my fault you packed all your shit without a word and left, taking three months to call?

"You left," I repeated for the second time, wanting him to feel the weight of his own decisions. We sat in silence, me looking away, biting my lip.

"I know," he said. "I want you back. You're the love of my life. I miss you."

Big sigh. Tears of joy. Hugs.

He agreed to counseling.

The biggest thing I learned during our sessions was that marriage is part of a three-way triangle. There's him, there's me, and there's the marriage. Think of the marriage as a third person; the counselor explained as he drew three points on a blank piece of paper, connecting the lines to form a triangle.

The marriage comes first, he told us, circling the dot at the top of the triangle. Everything you do as an individual affects the marriage (or third person). Considering every word or action and the effect it may have on the marriage is the key to making it work. I always thought of marriage being a partnership between two people. This was a new concept that our relationship was like a third person.

The counselor didn't sugarcoat his words. If we wanted our relationship to work, we had to put the third person (our marriage) first and make all our decisions based on what is best for the relationship. With the picture held in front of us, it was clear we both held responsibility for the state of our relationship. Humans are by nature selfish and self-centered, whether we realize it or care to admit it. That's what makes relationships and marriage challenging. We have to put the other person (relationship) before ourselves. In a healthy partnership, both people are active participants, balancing self and sacrifice. Sometimes you give, sometimes you take. Together, you create the rules of what that looks like.

Notice I said in a healthy relationship. It's like a teeter-totter. Ever ride one of those when you were a kid? In order for the teeter-totter to work, balance on both sides is required. If one person is too heavy or too light, the balance tips. If someone jumps off, there is no balance, no more fun. In fact, you can get injured if someone jumps off while you are in mid-air. The old saying is that it takes two to make or break a relationship. I say that's wrong. It takes two to make it work, but only one to break the bond. If someone jumps off or won't get on the teeter-totter, it can't work. If things are too far out of balance, either you are stuck up in the air or down on the ground by yourself.

We both wanted our marriage to work. We loved each other a great deal. What I discovered is that sometimes, that isn't enough. Where two people are in life, what they experienced growing up, and how emotionally healthy they are all play a significant part.

That was the second major lesson I learned. Some people are so entrenched in their habits and think they cannot (or will not) change without serious in-depth counseling. After meeting together and separately for a few sessions, my counselor told me the brutal truth. It was his opinion that my husband was incapable of change or of becoming a healthy partner unless he addressed deep hurts from his childhood. He was carrying wounds, stuck emotionally, and unable to function in a relationship. He also had extreme social anxiety, which was part of the past that followed him.

My husband made it clear he didn't want to do more counseling or dig into his past. He wanted to move home and begged me many times. I knew better, so I kept saying no. There had been no genuine change. It was my house. I bought it before we were married, so it was in my name. This gave me the upper hand on several levels. I called the shots. If our marriage was ever going to be healthy and happy, things had to change. I wanted a relationship with a partner I could rely on not to leave when things got tough. Someone I could talk to and share my most intimate thoughts and feelings with. A man I could lean on, trusting that he would be strong when I was weak. We both had things to work on. I was willing to do the emotional work, dig into the past and learn how to create a relationship built on mutual trust. Deep down, I believe he wanted that, too.

Wanting something and being able to accomplish it are two different things. That became another painful lesson. He begged to come home until he wore me down. Despite my better judgment, I let him move back in. It worked at first. Both of us were happy to be together, and we enjoyed a short honeymoon period. I stopped losing weight as soon as he returned. It took months for my body to replenish itself, but I looked and felt healthy again. If only we could fix our relationship that easily.

However, his moving back in only released the pressure valve; the steam escaped, removing the motivation to change, and it wasn't long before the same negative patterns emerged. His mode of dealing with things was silence. When my husband got mad, he didn't talk. In fact, if he was angry, you ceased to exist in his world. He walked right past me without acknowledging me, even though we lived in the same house. Weeks at a time passed without one word. I wouldn't know what I did to make him angry, but he punished me with silence. For someone that is a jabber mouth, living with a silent partner became a slow death. He carried grudges for a long time. Sometimes weeks or months, until he decided he wasn't mad anymore. It didn't matter if you spoke to him; he ignored you until he was darn good and ready to talk. I would never know why he was upset or how long I was to be shut out.

I begged him to talk to me, tell me what I did that made him so mad. It is impossible to fix your behavior if you don't know what triggers the other person. He would wring his hands, uncomfortable with the thought of discussing what he was feeling, and tell me he couldn't talk about it. Years of avoiding confrontation had worked for him until I came along. By then, the behavior grooves were deep, worn into his psyche. Digging out from the mire was more than he could handle. My openness became a threat. If he let go of his silence, it would force him to deal not only with my feelings but with his own. All my begging did was make him more distant.

When issues don't get resolved, they build up like an enormous pile of debris separating two people, one piece of garbage stacked on the next until resentment is all you feel. Frustration mounts higher and higher, and the stench of rotting waste overwhelms your senses, seeping into every corner of your heart. The love you once felt leaks out, leaving you cold, void of warmth or happiness. I learned from my counselor he used silence as a control tactic, and it destroyed our marriage. We ended up in separate bedrooms, leading our own lives, tension mounting between us.

No matter how many times I tried to get him to climb on the teeter-totter, he would jump off. I hit the ground a lot before I realized we would never find a balance. His issues went so deep that he wasn't capable of being in a relationship.

At least the cat was a bright spot. Jinx brought comfort to my daughter and me just by being there. Having a cat in the house felt normal. Our lives were far from normal, but at least the cat kept us on a routine. He needed to be fed and his litter box cleaned regularly, serving as an anchor in the restless sea of life. Calli held up her end of the bargain, taking care of the cat when she was home. Though, as a senior in high school, she was gone a lot, leaving me to do the extra tasks. My husband ignored Jinx, shutting him out behind a closed door as though he didn't exist, just like he did me.

Unlike my husband, Jinx was not silent. He enjoyed making his presence known. If he was unhappy, bored, or lonely, he let you know. Meowing loudly, often in the middle of the night, especially if Calli was gone. Racing through the house, scratching my wood floors with razor-sharp claws kept me both entertained and annoyed. Watching him slide across the floor, feet scurrying to stay upright, was amusing. If he was hungry, he would follow me around, insisting I feed him right now. Patience was not his virtue. When I ignored him, he would jump on the kitchen table, bathroom counter, or desk, knocking things off to get his way. As a last resort, he would swipe a paw at me as I passed, threatening to attack if I didn't heed his demands.

If I didn't understand what Jinx wanted, he used a new method to communicate. The cat was smart; I had to give him that. If he didn't get his way, he escalated his actions until they paid off. Only then did he retreat, relaxing in a quiet spot, curled up contentedly. Irritating communication was better than no communication in my book. Had my husband tried half as hard as the cat did, we might still be together. I made the right decision to get a cat, but I still wasn't sure that Jinx was the right choice.

Lesson number one learned: Cats are better than people.

LESSON #2:
SOMETIMES HATE TURNS INTO LOVE

All relationships go through a "honeymoon" period. In the beginning, everything seems perfect, and each party feels warm and fuzzy inside, at least until reality sets in months or years later like it did in my marriage. I never felt that with Jinx. I suppose my daughter did, but I don't recall feeling warm or fuzzy; just mad. The first night, he messed on a box of pictures behind her bed and scratched the neighbor's face when he tried picking Jinx up.

Then he terrorized my house. Clawing curtains, chairs, beds, anything available that he could dig his sharp claws into. The object of his highest affection was my favorite chair. I was in shock. Hobbs never acted that way, at least not that I remembered. She grew fat and lazy, so we called her Fat Cat. I wanted Fat Cat, not this Tasmanian devil, and I wondered why I ever brought this crazy cat home.

Jinx bullied Cleo, our dog, too. She was elderly and in poor health, and the cat ruled. Jinx would block her food bowl, acting like he was eating her food. If she tried to drink, he would rush to the water bowl, lapping until he had his fill, taking his sweet time until the dog understood his dominance. He took over the dog's bed, reclining like a king while Cleo slept on the floor.

I shooed him, chased him with a kitchen towel or a spray bottle, and yelled a lot. My attempts to dissuade him from destroying property only seemed to incite him to increase his efforts. So I stepped up my game too. Jinx would slink around the house, waiting for me to let my guard down, then rush in and attack some inanimate object with renewed ferocity. I'm sure he was laughing as he ran away.

Hatred ran rampant between us, and I devised ways of getting rid of this creature. It was easy to blame the cat for my problems. I'm sure he felt my pent-up frustration, the animosity often directed toward him instead of my husband. The cat didn't hide behind closed doors, though. He came out in the open, seeking my attention. Even if it was negative attention, it must have been better than no attention.

The answer to my problem came unexpectedly. My daughter announced when she turned eighteen that she was moving in with her boyfriend and taking the monster off my hands. Of course, it thrilled me to hear the cat would leave, but I was not ready for my daughter to exit.

She was my baby, the last of my three children. I figured I had at least six more months to prepare for an empty nest. If you have not experienced an empty nest, you can't understand the pain I was going through. I would lie on the floor in her bedroom, crying like a baby. There were reminders everywhere of the years spent together, not just from her but from all my children. Keepsakes gathering dust haunted me daily. Seashells gathered at the beach on vacation, layered in a glass jar. Rocks with odd shapes or interesting colors are proudly displayed along a windowsill. Clothes they had outgrown hung in the closet like ghosts. Once great treasures are now left behind without a thought. The sound of laughter, feet pounding up and down the stairs from an angry teenager, and the smell of too much cologne or perfume lingered in my memory. I longed for those days. I felt like a sad puppy, whining as the children ran off to school. Except they weren't coming back.

My marriage was dying, my babies were gone, and I was alone. I hurt deep inside, and it felt like the pain would never end. I spent twenty-six years raising kids, doing all the things moms do, and one day, it just stopped. Nobody needed me. It left me feeling like I wasn't a mom anymore, and I lost my identity.

Calli hadn't left the state, but she was as good as gone. She would rush in, grab something, and leave again. Then one night, she showed up with her bags and the cat. They had a fight. She needed to get away. Of course, you can stay here! At that point, I even welcomed Jinx. This back-and-forth game continued with her relationship. Each time she brought the cat home, he and I fought a little less until I missed the dang thing. Right?

Since I had so much time on my hands, I watched too much TV, and one night I caught the guy I call the cat whisperer (Jackson Galaxy). He fixes feline behavior issues and sometimes the owners are the ones that need fixing. It couldn't be that I needed fixing, could it? After watching a couple of shows, I realized my house was not very cat friendly. I bought more scratching posts, put one in every room, and found interactive cat toys. Jackson is big on playing with your cat every day as it bonds the owner with the cat and releases its natural prey drive. It was apparent that this cat had a lot of prey drive.

Wherever Jinx scratched, I placed a carpeted scratching post there with a little cat nip sprinkled on the base. I purchased another cat tower for the window after learning that most cats like to be high above the ground. Things took a positive turn. I invited him onto my lap, allowing him to share my beloved chair. He reminded me of how calming it was to stroke a purring cat. His long fur was soft, a bonus in disguise. His body curled up next to me, warming not only my lap but also my heart.

Jinx and I quit playing our cat-and-mouse game. I stopped directing my anger at him, and he stopped terrorizing me. Once I did that, we sort of became friends.

We worked out little compromises. Like, my chair is for me, the matching footstool is for you. Unless I invited him on my lap, I didn't allow him into my chair, but the footstool was all his. He had an uncanny ability to figure out where the boundaries were, and, mostly; he respected them. Our understanding of each other grew, and dare I say; we became fond of one another.

After a multitude of fights between Calli and her boyfriend that ended with her dragging Jinx from one house to the next, Calli announced, "Mom, Jinx is happier with you. I think you need to keep him."

"What?" I asked in disbelief as Jinx rolled belly up on the floor and purred at my feet.

"Yeah, look at him. He's more relaxed here. I can't take good care of him."

Here was the cat I had despised, and now, warmth filled my heart to hear those words. I knew my daughter was right. She had contemplated the situation before she said anything. If she asked me to keep Jinx, she was sacrificing herself for his well-being. Then she announced she was leaving the state, her boyfriend (and me).

"If I take him, Calli, he's mine, so be sure."

With tears in her eyes, she said goodbye to Jinx and left him in my care.

There is a distinction between cat sitting and cat ownership. Cat sitting is temporary; cat ownership is permanent. I was now a cat owner, and I took it seriously.

Episodes of My Cat from Hell played in the house as I learned as much as I could about cat behavior. Jinx was not your typical cat, and if we were going to live together, I needed to be informed. I realized Jinx had changed nothing. Understanding why he acted the way he did helped me change my behavior. As I calmed down, gave him the attention he desired, and adapted to his surroundings to accommodate the needs of a cat instead of insisting he lived like a human, we developed a strong bond.

I got over the grief of an empty nest in about six months. After 26 years of raising children, I realized my life was mine. I didn't have to cook, clean or grocery shop nearly as often. I could come and go as I wished, eat what I wanted, and leave town on a whim. There were no more teacher conferences or school events to attend. No waiting up at night to make sure they made it home, worrying every time the phone rang past ten o'clock. The joy of my newfound freedom replaced the misery of an empty nest.

All my studying of cat behavior paid off, resulting in a peaceful co-existence with Jinx. The cat was there to greet me when I came home, waiting by the door with happy meows. He kept me company, gave me lots of "cat therapy," sat on my lap, and allowed me to pet him for long periods of time. We settled into a comfortable routine. I fed him at the same time each day, cleaned his box, and we relaxed together in the evening.

He released his hold over the dog, allowing Cleo to eat in peace, eventually sharing the pet bed with her. As she grew weaker, Jinx spent most of his time curled beside her, his presence calming her. They became inseparable, touching noses, Jinx following Cleo around as though he were her nurse.

I don't know how we would have survived without that pesky pet. He filled the house with activity, kept me from going bat-shit crazy, and gave me a reason to come home. The cat I once hated was now my friend. He had befriended my daughter, my dog, and now me.

Lesson number two learned: Sometimes hate turns into love.

LESSON #3:
CHANGE IS PART OF LIFE

I thought I was done with harsh life lessons, at least for a while. Turns out there was more to learn. A shadowy enemy was hiding, waiting for the right time to strike.

Amid the chaos of the last eight months, I also started a new career in the health insurance industry, which pushed my stress levels off the charts. It took me several months of intense study while working a full-time job to pass the state test.

Jinx and I spent weekends, evenings, and lunch hours hitting the books. He would recline at my feet, under my home office desk, or curl up on my lap, purring away. When he decided we were done, he'd jump up on the desk, knock my pencil or some minor item off, reminding me it was dinnertime. Jinx is the most persistent cat I have ever met. When he wants something, he will stop at nothing to get his way. I wanted a new career, and insurance seemed to offer the opportunity I was looking for. Watching him was a great lesson in perseverance, encouraging me not to give up.

Remembering the information was more challenging than I'd expected. Never someone that liked to study, so it took me months to get through the thick, boring book. When I felt ready to take the test, I traveled two hours one way in the wee hours of the morning to sit for the exam at an official testing site. I was beyond nervous during the two-hour test. Statistics show that most people don't pass the first time. It was not a simple test, at least for me. One hundred fifty questions, worded in tricky ways, took concentration and reasoning. The ride home was nerve-racking, wondering if I had passed.

I scored an 89%, higher than I expected and well above the 70% needed to pass. It was a proud day when I received my Life, Health, and Accident License. My friends helped me celebrate with dinner and a toast to my new career.

Now it was time to find a job in the insurance field. I didn't just want a job; I wanted a career. Things were going well in my current position as a hotel sales director, where I'd been for 6 years. The money was good, but the stress was draining. Tight deadlines, high pressure, and a boss that resembled Miranda Priestly in The Devil Wears Prada pushed me to a breaking point. She was a brilliant businesswoman but a terrible boss. Personal attacks became a daily occurrence. Either she wouldn't acknowledge your presence, or she'd make a snide remark about how you looked or what you wore, not just toward me but also anyone that came in contact with her.

On the flip side, she was highly intelligent, a shrewd negotiator, and quick to reward excellence. I learned a great deal from her during my time of employment. She gave me the opportunity to create my job from the beginning, providing me with the time and support to establish a firm basis in my work that helped us both for a long time. She invested money to improve my sales skills, sending me to the best training I ever received, changing my future and hers. When the company made money from my efforts, she made sure I did too. My confidence grew, along with my bank account, allowing me to buy a house as a single mom.

I handled the convention/reunion side of the hotel business; she was in charge of the bus tours. Together, we were a powerful force. She could take on an amazing amount of work and assumed everyone around her could, too. The rest of us ran as hard and fast as we could, trying to keep up, often leading to frazzled nerves and burnout. There was a large turnover in her office. Few people could handle the pace or her demeanor.

I had an assistant, drove a company car, got to travel to conventions around the country, and enjoyed fat paychecks. But it was time to move on. The honeymoon was over, the pressure too much after 6 years under her thumb. Now I had a picture of what I could do, how much I could earn.

All I needed was the right opportunity. In our small town, opportunities were rare, so I created my own. I looked into owning a franchise, such as State Farm, but I lacked the funds needed to get started; back to working for someone. It was quite serendipitous when an ad for a Blue Cross Blue Shield group agent appeared in the local newspaper just weeks after receiving my license.

It was a big job and one that didn't come along often in small-town Wyoming. It offered a company car, significant benefits, a salary, and the ability to earn six figures. At the peak of my confidence, there was no doubt I could handle it. If I could survive and thrive under Cruella De Vil, I could do this.

I've never been very good at handling stress, especially when starting a new job. Not knowing what I was doing, learning new tasks, and the uncomfortableness of being in a new place with unfamiliar people caused me great anxiety. As an over-achiever, I worked long hours to learn three unique computer programs. One program used the archaic DOS system. I didn't start using computers until Windows came along, so it was like learning a new language. My work often took me out of town, driving long distances for training or meeting customers within a 300-mile radius. I hate driving. I can make myself car sick driving on a winding road. Sitting for endless hours, cramped in a car, gave me chronic back pain. Tight schedules and pressure to sell health insurance plans I barely understood while delivering bad news of increased group rates left me miserable. The more unhappy I became, the less confident I was.

Salespeople must believe in what they are selling. If they don't believe in their product, why would their customers buy it? My former boss told people I could sell ice to an Eskimo. This time, I didn't believe in what I was selling. I often had to deliver the bad news of higher rates or denied policies. My drive to succeed overcame my fear, and I pressed on. Until the monster hiding in the shadows hunted me down.

It was barely noticeable at first. A few hours of missed sleep didn't seem like a big deal. The nervousness was normal since I had gone through some major life changes. That's what I told myself. Until the few hours of missed sleep turned into full-blown insomnia, and the nervousness became overwhelming anxiety. Imagine a world where you are awake 24-7 with no sleep. The nights become endless, stretching out like a long highway that never ends. You drive, day and night but never arrive. There is no destination, no hotels, no rest areas, just an endless highway. You grow weary, your eyes heavy, your body begging you to stop, but you can't. All you can do is drive. Now imagine it's dark, with below-zero temperatures, howling winds, and a desolate landscape void of sunlight. That was my reality in the winter of 2012.

Did anxiety lead to insomnia, or did insomnia lead to anxiety? No one seemed to have the answer. I was on a merry-go-round, spinning out of control. Anxiety, insomnia, depression, anxiety, insomnia, depression, round and round I went. Someone, or something, was controlling me, and I couldn't stop it. I tried putting my foot down, dragging the earth to slow down. I wanted to jump off, but I was going too fast. Dizziness, confusion, and hopelessness swirled in my head until my grasp on reality blurred, passing rapidly around me.

One missed appointment sent me over the cliff. How could I be so stupid? Didn't I have a calendar? Use it, dummy. Doubts crept in, and dark clouds floated down, settling in like a thick fog.

I can't do this. I'm not smart enough.
This is too much. I'll never learn.
I hate this job.

There was a lot on the line. My career, my self-respect, my family, and my pride. All counted on me to succeed. I'd told my boss I could do this and reassured him I was the one for the job. He wouldn't need to babysit me. Once I learned the job, he'd rarely have to check-in. That was true before I landed on the stress merry-go-round.

I made three times as much money as my husband, carried a mortgage, had a child in college, one graduating high school, and had a reputation to uphold. At my last company, I traveled around the country, gave presentations to 300 people, and sold 3 times as much as any other salesperson. I was the Rotary club president, a reliable mom, and a faithful friend. That's who I was.

This person was dumb. She couldn't do anything right. She failed to show up for appointments, let people down, whined, and was ineffective. She was a failure. Demons whispered dark secrets in my ear, telling me how unworthy I was, how stupid I was, and that no one liked me anymore.

Despite a stack of sold policies, others telling me they appreciated my simple explanation of insurance terms, and my boss reassuring me, I believed the worst.

At the end of each day, I returned home to Jinx. He was the bright spot in my dark days. He was glad to see me, listened when I whined, and was there when I fell apart. If I sobbed the moment I walked through the door, there was no judgment from him. I could be a wreck, and he still wanted to be with me. He purred with happiness to be in my lap, curled beside me as the sleepless nights droned on. Jinx was my anchor in the storm. I didn't have to pretend I was OK with him.

My soul grew dark. All hope seeped away like the light on a winter day. The sun set on my life, taking any warmth, happiness, or purpose I felt. I was cold inside. I couldn't laugh or smile. There was no joy left. Someone had sucked the life out of me, leaving me in a puddle on the floor, devoid of form or substance. I have a vivid recollection of standing in front of the television in my living room, my hands trembling. I froze with fear, anxiety, and self-doubt and had a nervous breakdown.

I didn't realize that's what it was until much later. My mind shut down; my body responded to protect me. It had been trying to tell me, but I didn't listen. There was no more pretending. I couldn't face one more day at the office. I resigned and quit my new career. Everything I had worked so hard for was gone. The hours of studying, the satisfaction I felt when I got the job, and the future I envisioned slipped through my fingers, and there was nothing I could do to stop it.

Tell me how someone capable of traveling the country and presenting to 300 people becomes unable to go to the grocery store. It made little sense to me, either. Not only did I not comprehend what happened, but I also hid away, ashamed, unable to talk about what I was going through. Only my closest friends and family knew of my condition.

My husband and I were still together, but he was no help. He wasn't unable to cope with our relationship when things were good; he was useless when things went bad. He stayed in his room, isolated from me or my problems. His world comprised work, TV (set up in his room), and going to the gym.

My condition went undiagnosed, despite seeing my doctor, a psychiatrist, and an alternative medicine person. They prescribed sleeping pills, anxiety meds, antidepressants, and herbal formulas. I changed my diet for three months (no sugar, no alcohol, and low carbohydrates) but nothing helped. Of course, I was depressed and had anxiety. That much was clear to everyone but me. I focused solely on not being able to sleep because that was a living hell. But what was the cause? No one could tell me.

When you cannot sleep for weeks at a time, the days never end. It's like being a hamster on a wheel that goes round and round. Except I could not stop the spinning or get off the wheel. The trembling stopped on the outside but continued on the inside. It coursed through me, like an electrical current, jolting me awake. The nights were long and torturous. Sleep eluded me, except for short periods here and there when I would doze off, only to wake within minutes. I would lie there, hour after hour, begging, praying, hoping for some rest.

The sound of my mother's voice was the only thing that calmed me. I called her at all hours of the night, and she would read to me. Sometimes she read the bible, or an excerpt from a book or newspaper article. It didn't matter. As long as I could hear her, I would relax until one of us gave in to slumber. She was selfless, sacrificing her own rest for me. I always knew my mom loved me, but during that time, I realized just how deep her love was.

My oldest brother, Jeff, had experienced something similar after an explosion near his ear left him with severe tinnitus, leaving him unable to sleep. He called me often, speaking words of hope. Few people understood what I was going through, knowing he cared, that he was there for me, helped a great deal.

He kept telling me, "You will get better. This will pass. Don't give up."

We were never close growing up; he was four years older and detached from his little sister. My tragedy brought us closer. It was the start of a close bond I am grateful for, and it changed our relationship.

I became suicidal, and at one point, my mom called the police to check on me. Embarrassed and unable to lift myself out of the deep depression, all I could do was survive. My life was void of laughter, joy, and happiness. I couldn't even smile. My soul was leaving my body. I didn't wear makeup, perfume, or jewelry. I had no sex drive, got no pleasure from food or drink, and cared for nothing and no one.

Friends and family got me through that long winter, and of course, Jinx, my cat therapist. He sensed my turmoil, lying close to me, sending his warmth into my body. Staying on the couch with me all night as I watched mind-numbing TV, curled up on my lap, purring. An avid reader, I couldn't even enjoy my favorite pastime. The words became jumbled; the story made little sense, and I couldn't concentrate. Any darkness or death in a show became magnified, filling me with fear and dread and sending me back into my cave. My memory was fragmented. I'd forget what you asked for or told me moments ago.

Friends brought me food and drug me out of the house. They planned and hosted Calli's high school graduation party, something I could not handle. Pictures taken during that time showed a face void of life. A blank look in my eyes, as though my soul was gone.

With time, the trembling stopped, and I could function on a low level, enough to get a meaningless job doing simple tasks. I'd gone from a high-level position, making close to $80,000 a year, into a puddle on the floor in less than six months. Misery surrounded me. To say I was depressed was an understatement. Not knowing why was the hardest part. I just couldn't understand what had happened.

With time, I got better, and life returned to semi-normal. We all thought it was severe depression caused by the major life events that occurred in quick succession. But when the anxiety returned a few months later, I knew it was more than depression. Fear filled me, knowing that insomnia would soon follow. I racked my brain, trying to figure out what the caveat was. Had I changed anything? Done anything different?

One day I was fine. The next, I was spiraling downhill again. The season was the only thing different. There it was, glaring at me, and it made sense. Seasonal Affective disorder (SAD).

When the hours of daylight diminished with the fall and winter seasons, it triggered my depression, anxiety, and insomnia. My condition went undiscovered because my symptoms were the opposite of most people with SAD. Instead of sleeping too much, I wasn't able to sleep at all. That, added to all the stress and heartbreak I experienced in a short period, resulted in my condition.

Since I knew what was wrong, I could fix it. There were plenty of articles on the internet, and I devoured the information. Something changes in the brain chemistry of those with SAD, and the biological clock that regulates moods, sleep, and hormones, shifts, causing us to be out of step with our daily schedule. We can't adjust to the changes in daylight length.

Uneducated but well-meaning friends and family don't understand. It's not a matter of making up our minds or having a better attitude. It's physiological, and we have no control over it. For me, it was the perfect storm. All things collided at one time. A series of unfortunate events, one on top of the next, exploded in my life. Telling me to get it together, stay positive, or it's all in my mind, was not helpful. Being positive wasn't enough. Saying depression is a symptom of repressed anger, so if you figure out why you are angry, then you can deal with it wasn't helpful.

Yeah, I was angry. Mad at the world during that time. Years of undealt with emotions, poor decisions, and perfectionism piled up, but it was the SAD that tipped me over the edge. Had I known it was hiding in the corner, waiting to attack, I might have avoided the crash. No one knew or suspected. It wasn't the root cause, but it magnified everything, resulting in near-death for me.

Once the enemy had hold of my life, it strangled me. Left untreated, I believe I would have ended up in a mental institution. I couldn't believe how quickly the enemy stripped me of my ability to function.

The flip of a switch was about to set me free. All I had to do was change one thing. The common theme in managing my mood disorder was light therapy (phototherapy), which involves specialized lights designed to deliver a therapeutic dose of bright light to treat symptoms. I ordered one as fast as I could. Since my symptoms are abnormal, it took trial and error before I found what worked for me. For most people, sitting under such a bright light stimulates them, so they recommend 20-30 minutes in the morning, but I discovered it relaxed me, and I could fall asleep within minutes of being exposed to the rays, so I added the light routine in the evening.

After years of adjusting, I now mimic summer daylight hours with my light therapy, using at least 30 minutes in the morning and 30 minutes in the evening (6 AM and 9 PM). Sometimes I also use the light during the day in the fall, winter, or even overcast days.

At the time of my breakdown, I was living in Wyoming. Their winters are freezing, with bitter icy winds and short daylight hours. Even with my light therapy, I was unhappy, and my anxiety remained. The place I once loved and thrived in became a prison. Summer lasted three months if you were lucky. It was no longer enough for me. I needed a sunnier climate, somewhere closer to the equator. Life up north no longer worked, and it was time to change my life. I imagined what it would be like with more sunshine, longer days, and a warmer climate. The only thing holding me back was the man in my house, who was no husband at all. We existed together, but there was no intimacy, communication, or trust. Talking about moving sent him into anxiety, and he withdrew further. When I needed a partner to carry me through or walk beside me, he was the most distant. Retreating to his room or going to work, avoiding contact and conversation. My life had transitioned from being a mom to being an empty nester. He wouldn't discuss it or let me express my feelings. A closed door was the answer I received.

My career died, taking my income with it. My body and brain were healing, but I was not ready to handle a stressful workload. I worked a depressing job in a basement office for a chiropractor. Day in and day out, I witnessed bodies destroyed by accidents, work, or poor health. I saw people in excruciating pain, some unable to get out of their vehicles. Grown men brought to their knees with back pain, cried for relief. To me, the basement was like a dungeon, the lack of daylight making my SAD even worse. I brought home less pay than my husband did, had no medical benefits, and trudged through life like I did the snow.

I loved my husband a great deal, despite all the pain and suffering we went through, but the desire for a new life was stronger than my feelings. I wanted a help-mate. Someone I could talk to, lean on, and walk beside through whatever life threw at us. After you have been to hell and back, things look different. I was different. Accepting the life that led to my destruction was no longer an option. Wyoming symbolized death to me, like the lifeless landscape in the winter.

Love covers a multitude of sins, and I forgave him again and again. That did not fix him or our relationship. I learned to see my love for him as a gift. For the first time, I knew what it was to truly love a man with all my heart. No matter what happened or what he did or didn't do, I felt love. The hardest lesson I ever learned is that sometimes, love isn't enough.

When the frustration from being left to deal with things alone spilled over, I screamed, cried, and begged him to talk to me. The anger felt better than acting like everything was fine. At least I was expressing my feelings. All it did was give him an excuse to retreat, locking himself in his room and avoiding me or conflict. At the height of my frustration, I followed him, screaming insults, as he retreated to his room, slamming the door in my face. My fist pounded on the door as I screamed, "You big f&*$#@! baby! Come out and act like a man." Not my finest moment.

My wise friend Margie asked me why I was so angry at him for being who he was.

"People are where they are, Cyn. He's just being who is," she said. "His methods have worked for him until now. He has to see what could be different and decide to change it himself. You being angry won't change him. He's stuck, right where he is, unless he decides to be somewhere else."

"So, what can I do?"

"You can only control your reaction. You either accept him the way he is or leave."

The realization that I could not control him or anything he did was monumental. She was right. Nothing I did or said was going to change him. I hoped and prayed he would decide to work on himself.

One thing was for sure: I couldn't stay in Wyoming any longer. My mental and physical health dictated I make a change or I would surely die. By the grace of God, I would not spend another winter in the north. Still, my heart held on to the belief that we could make things work.

I looked at sunny places to live that might suit my husband. He loved to fish and hunt, so I presented options that offered more sunshine for me and outdoor sports for him. He hated his job and wanted to move, but he would not discuss our options. A major life change was too much for him. He was, as Margie said, stuck. I, however, needed to get the hell out of there.

Fear and excitement swirled around me. Jinx sensed my renewed energy, following me around, meowing when I talked to him. I researched places I wanted to live. Somewhere with fun and sun, with similarities to Wyoming. Jinx seemed interested in the places I researched, listening as I carried on about the virtues of each, biting my pencil eraser as I scribbled notes. He brushed against the computer screen, stepped on my keyboard, and walked across the desk as though he understood what I was doing.

"Jinx, would you like to live here?" I'd ask, pointing to pictures of various towns and cities.

We gazed at landscapes and population guides, studied the weather and climates, and looked for maximum days of sunshine. Until we were more confused than ever. It was impossible to know what an area was like unless you visited, but there was little room for travel in my budget.

My oldest daughter, Brandie, suggested Flagstaff, Arizona. She was living there after graduating from NAU (Northern Arizona University). I visited her several times and enjoyed the place. It had mountains (sort of), sunny days with proximity to warmer climates, and outdoor adventures galore. Fun pictures with her friends filled her Facebook page. Young people living their lives to the fullest. That's what I wanted, to live a full life.

A brief visit to Flagstaff, staying with my daughter to save costs, allowed me to consider the area from a new perspective. My husband refused to take the trip with me, so I went alone. At first, I was anxious, flooded with fear of leaving a life I'd known for 30 years. This was uncomfortable, trying to decide in a few days if I should move. What if I made the wrong decision? Brandie's boyfriend chauffeured us around like a couple of ladies-in-waiting. Together they showed me neighborhoods, took me through the college campus, and walked me downtown to get a sense of the culture, the food, and the people. It was a far cry from the conservative cowboy culture I was used to.

Bright colors and earthy smells emanated from the local shops. Farm-to-table restaurants, bars, and cobblestones lined the main street. Dogs greeted me happily on almost every corner. They were allowed in most places, inside or out, as long as they were on a leash and well-behaved. Crystals hung in shop windows along with peace signs. Patchouli and lavender tickled my nose. Coffee shops with signature alcoholic drinks, a tea house, outdoor sporting goods stores, and art galleries made up downtown. There were pizza places, hidden speakeasies, outdoor patios, and musicians performing for tips thrown into empty guitar cases, competing for sidewalk space. I tried not to stare. It felt like I was on another planet, and I just stepped out the door for the first time. If it was a change I wanted, this place was perfect.

A drive through the Wind River Canyon sealed the deal. Looking at the beauty along the river, watching people gear up for hiking and biking, and imagining it was me heading out for an adventure helped me decide. I knew this was where my new life would begin. It had everything I dreamed of. A warmer climate, sunny days even in winter, and hiking and biking trails galore. I was no longer afraid.

My husband enjoyed mountain biking. He was the one that got me started, surprising me with a new bike on my birthday. Unlike me, he liked to hunt, especially elk. Much to my surprise, Flagstaff had elk. It offered wide open spaces, pine trees, rivers for fishing, and fresh air. All the things he enjoyed. I was sure he would love it if only he would give it a chance. It seemed like the perfect compromise. Hunting and fishing for him, sunshine for me, mountain biking for us both.

When I returned from my trip, I put my house up for sale. I tried talking to my husband, hoping to persuade him to join me. I wanted to tell him a place existed that offered us both what we wanted. After all, I'd been through, he had to realize I couldn't stay in Wyoming. He wouldn't listen, didn't want to hear what I had to say. The day the for-sale sign appeared in the yard, he removed his wedding band, asked for a divorce, and walked out the door.

I filed for divorce after several attempts to discuss the matter. He insisted, wringing his hands, that divorce was what he wanted. I knew he would never file the papers or fight for anything. If I was leaving, starting a new life, it made sense to complete things before I left. He got what was his; I took what was mine; he signed willingly. It wasn't what I wanted. I loved him with my whole heart, but I knew I couldn't stay. That would have been emotional and physical suicide.

Tears streamed down my face as I stood at the courthouse desk. The lady behind the counter knew me since it was a small town. She knew I had been married and divorced before. Yet, she was non-judgmental. Her eyes showed empathy. It was clear I was in a great deal of pain.

When I got home, my dog, Cleo, lay on the floor in her own excrement, unable to move. I knew her passing was imminent, but I didn't expect I would have to put her to sleep today. Of all days, this could happen. Why today? I loaded her into the car and called my husband. He refused to go with me or have any part in it. He loved the dog more than I did, but he simply could not deal with this. So, I did it alone. Pain, anger, and frustration all poured out when the vet came to my car and helped my dog pass in peace. I wept uncontrollably.

That was one of the worst days of my life. My three best friends were there for me. Margie, Lisa, and Leslie rallied around, took me out to eat, and presented me with a sweet gift. Thank God for friends. Life had to get better, right?

When I walked into the dark house that night, drained of emotion, Jinx was there. Sitting in the kitchen, waiting for me, the outline of his furry felineness a welcoming sight.

"It's me and you, Jinx, against the world," I said. "I hope you're ready."

I remembered the first day I saw him in the shelter, the scraggly cat I never wanted. Here I was, talking to him like he was my best friend. His life changed the day we brought him home, and so did mine. Life was about to change again. Calli moved out. Cleo was gone. My marriage was over. Jinx was the only thing that remained steady through it all. Little did I know, he would be my constant companion through a lot more change. There is something about going through hard times together when all you can count on is each other that strengthens a bond.

He meowed as I reached down to pet him. I'd learned he doesn't like to be picked up, but he loves to have his neck scratched. I plopped down on the floor beside him and drew comfort from the soft drumming of his purr. The cat I once chased away was now the friend I needed to help me through this change.

True to my word, I left Wyoming that spring. I packed my stuff and said goodbye to long-time friends. It was bittersweet, leaving a place I'd loved so much. To help me transition, I asked for a farewell party.

I'd been reading a book called "Transitions," by William Bridges. A friend had gifted me the book to help during this time. It stressed the importance of ceremonies during a transition. I was about to make one of the biggest transitions in my life. Anything I could do to ease the change was worth trying, I reasoned. Bridges points to our lack of ceremonial events in the modern world as part of why we struggle with change. Recognizing when you are in transition and the three stages you are likely to experience can ease the discomfort. He points out that societies that still celebrate life events, such as the passing from childhood to adulthood, fare much better than our fast-paced modern society, where we have largely moved away from these types of ceremonies.

Something as simple as a going-away party might help me (and my friends) with closure. My current life had to die before my new life could begin. The party would signal the closure of one life, the start of a new one. Before reading the book, I never really understood a farewell party. In the past, it irritated me that people waited until someone was leaving to bring out cake, cards, and kind words. Now it made sense.

Surrounded by people I loved, some I had known for many years, others only a few, we laughed, cried, reminisced, and finally toasted my departure. The transition had begun. I knew I would always be friends with some of them. Their wisdom, kindness, and love would go with me, if only in my heart.

My husband and I never said goodbye. He was still living in the house when I left since we had agreed he would stay until it sold. It allowed him time to find other living arrangements, which he was not in a hurry to do. He was gone the day my friend Jocko helped load the truck. The day prior, he left early for work, locked himself in his room when he came home and never spoke a word to me. His wedding band was still on the counter when I walked out the door for the last time.

The weekend before Mother's Day, I arrived in sunny Arizona. Jinx traveled in a crate on the seat beside me in a 14 ft. U-Haul. My knuckles were white, driving that beast while towing my car behind. But we made it together and arrived in blue skies, mild temps, and glorious sunshine!

Jinx is the only cat I have ever met that loves his crate. Most felines I dealt with would not enter the perceived death trap without a herculean effort. Not Jinx. Open the crate, put it on the floor, and he walks right in. Maybe it's curiosity that draws him into the crate, or it represents safety and security. His willingness to enter the crate proved especially helpful during our quest. One less thing for me to worry about.

Watching Jinx enter his crate, not knowing where he would end up once the door opened, was a lesson in trust. I did not know what my life was going to be like in Flagstaff. That was part of the fun and the fear. But Jinx was with me, and we would soon find out if I made the right decision.

Lesson number three learned: Change is part of life.

LESSON #4:
WE ARE NOT IN CONTROL (ESPECIALLY WITH CATS)

When I moved to Arizona, I didn't have a place to live because nobody would rent to me until I arrived. My hotel was an extended stay, budget-friendly place. One of those sleazy places where you fear being carried off by roaches when you turn out the lights. I needed to find somewhere to hang my hat, fast.

Flagstaff, Arizona, is a beautiful spot with mountains, crystal clear skies, and outdoor adventure galore. A college town filled with trust fund babies and an infrastructure lacking sufficient housing leads to high prices. So things are expensive. To survive the exorbitant rent, those without ample means share housing, up to six or seven people together, which is not uncommon. This was no surprise to me. I knew what I was getting myself into, and I was ready. Funny how things don't bother you when you decide they won't. Here I was, 49 years young, prepared to live with roommates like I was the one in college.

By the time I moved to Flagstaff, my daughter, Brandie, had graduated and was long gone. Except for Mr. Jinx, I was alone. No one to worry about. I was in control of my own life, and it felt good. I found several rooms for rent in a large house on the golf course and moved into the one with a small patio overlooking the greens. They furnished it with a big four-poster bed and a desk. Perfect, I thought. Just enough space for Jinx and me. It was a big house, so Jinx would have lots of rooms to explore. I couldn't keep him shut up in my little space. After all, he was an adventurer and never happy unless he was venturing.

The owners seemed normal at first. A couple in their mid-fifties, she was outgoing and friendly; he was more reserved but pleasant enough. They had two yappy dogs, a mixture of Pomeranian and Yorkshire terrier.

The problem was those two dogs kept Jinx confined. As soon as he tried to leave my bedroom, they went on high alert and chased him back to my room. Not only did the dogs terrorize Jinx, but they had other bad habits, like messing on the floor wherever they wanted. Puddles showed up in very inconvenient places.

We had lived there for about a week when I noticed they had moved my things. Someone was entering my room when I was absent. Paying my rent came with an expectation that my room was private, the common areas were for everyone, but the bedrooms were off-limits. It was time for a talk.

I was pretty sure it was her doing the snooping. She was the odd duck and was home all day, so I confronted her. She didn't deny it and agreed to stay clear of my room unless invited. Good, I thought, problem solved.

It took things one week to go from bad to worse. The dogs and lack of privacy made me want to leave, but the next incident left me no choice. I came home late one night, wanting a cup of chamomile tea before going to bed. The pot was on the stove, whistling away when she freaked out. There was a staircase perpendicular to the kitchen that led to the second floor where she and her husband lived. She was half-naked, peering over the railing, screaming her bloody head off at the sight of me by the stove. Luckily, she raced upstairs and not toward me.

Another confrontation was necessary.

"Last night when I came home, and you screamed at me, that was unsettling. If you're going to freak out every time I come home past 10 at night, this will never work," I said.

"What?" she said, surprised.

"You don't remember standing on the stairs, screaming?" I asked.

"No. I didn't hit you, did I?" she asked with concern in her voice.

My mind reeled. She said that with conviction, as though it was a real possibility.

"No…" I answered, shaking my head and staring at her.

"Oh, well, that's good," she replied.

She apologized and mumbled something about sleepwalking. That conversation started a rapid search for a new place to live. Good thing my lease was month to month! I dug out the paperwork and read the fine print. All I needed to do was give a week's notice. Thank God.

You can't imagine the chaos that ensued in the next 7 days. The morning would start out normal when I was in the kitchen making myself breakfast. She was pleasant enough until about noon. I'd hear the clink of ice and the freezer door slam, and before long, she was slurring her words, weaving back and forth with a glass in her hand. She'd start screaming at her husband, yelling obscenities. The dogs scattered. He made himself scarce, and still, I could hear her carry on. Bitching him out constantly.

"Ralph, did you do this?"

"Ralph, why didn't you do that?"

"Ralph, where are you?"

What was in the freezer? I snuck into the kitchen early the next day to find out. There were several full bottles of the clear stuff. The big ones. I'm naïve, I guess; I didn't realize people kept vodka in the freezer. By the next day, there was only one bottle left. Wow, a fifth of vodka disappeared overnight. She was a drunk. A blackout, not remembering anything she did while drinking, drunk. The screaming and lack of recollection made sense. I also found out that the man she called her husband was her ex-husband.

She let me in on their "secret" one night when she drank too much. She was watching me cook my dinner, tipping her glass of vodka until the ice slid past her mouth, a few pieces falling on the floor.

"He's my ex-husband, you know," she said.

"Oh?" I replied.

"Yeah, we got divorced a couple of years ago. But he came crawling back."

She slumped in her chair with no bra, her hair a mess, and her face swollen from too much vodka. I couldn't imagine why anyone would come back for more of that.

The next day, the FBI showed up at the door to question my landlords. Then the washer overflowed, flooding the basement because she filled it too full. I guess it's hard to judge such things when you drink a fifth of vodka. Every day, it was a fresh disaster. She created it; he fixed it. It was a great relationship dynamic.

The last straw came when the two devil dogs chased Jinx into my bedroom and cornered him under the bed. Good thing I kept a broom handy. She was next if she stepped one foot in here.

How could I be so stupid? Here I was, living in hell again, by my own dumb decision. I called Margie.

"What is wrong with me?" I asked, distraught.

She is the ultimate optimist, wise beyond belief, and full of grace. She's like a modern-day guru.

"No, Cyn, you're not stupid. This was only a placeholder. The perfect place is coming. It just wasn't quite ready. Believe it," she said.

Margie always made me feel better. I sighed, trying to believe.

I had given my weeks' notice before having a new place to live. It was now day four, and still nothing. Remember, housing is limited and expensive, and I had a cat, making my search even harder. Jinx was now part of me, and where I went, he went. No exceptions, so I kept searching.

That evening I met a new acquaintance for dinner and bowling. I didn't know what a "Meet-up" group was prior to Flagstaff. My oldest daughter told me to Google "Meet-ups in Flagstaff" to find like-minded folks looking to make new friends or share adventures. Turns out they have groups for almost anything, especially in a college town. Socializing, hiking, dancing… you post an event, and people just show up. That's how I met Christina, the sweet gal sitting across from me. We were going to dinner and then bowling. It was fortuitous that I was the only one that arrived. I spilled my story over a local IPA and pizza.

She hesitated, then said.

"I have a friend in my apartment complex that might want a roommate. She has two-bedrooms and might appreciate the help with rent. I'll text her."

I bought dinner to show my appreciation. By the time we bowled our second game, I had connected with the girl in apartment 203. We met the next day after work. Janella was in her late 20s, dark-haired, Spanish speaking but with almost perfect English. She was lovely, warm, and seemed normal enough. She didn't like cats much, though.

"Jinx is no regular cat. He's more like a dog. He's super smart, loves people and I'm sure you'll like him," I said with my best smile, flashing her a picture of Jinx.

The first of the month was still 2 days away. I could move in on Monday. Today was Friday. The thought of staying in the crazy house for another 24 hours was horrifying. I must have looked desperate because Janella offered to let me move in over the weekend. She was leaving town anyway, and we could complete the paperwork on Monday, she said, handing me a spare key. She would need a place to store things in order to accommodate me, though. I offered my newly rented storage unit; we could share the space and the cost. It was a perfect match right from the beginning.

I've never packed as fast as I did that weekend. By Saturday morning at 10 AM, Jinx and I settled in our new place. There was a small, fenced-in porch looking out at the forest, furnished with a lounge chair, a side table, and a small grill. That evening I poured myself a cold beer, cooked a grass-fed burger, and enjoyed the view. My best life had begun.

It cost me a $500 deposit and an extra $50 a month in rent to have Jinx. I forked it over. Small price for happiness, I thought.

Janella and I spent the next couple of weeks getting to know one another. We hiked, talked for hours, and drank lots of local beer. I was a decorator by trade, so I inspired her to upgrade our surroundings. We scoured the second-hand shops, looking for treasures, shopped for new curtains, and worked together to create a cozy space we called home.

When riding with her, I discovered she had road rage. She found out about my SAD. Janella hated mornings. I loved them. We were both nursing a broken heart, and after drinking enough beer, we cried together. Sometimes we switched to red wine when the weather got too cold for a beer.

At first, Janella avoided Jinx. It took him a while to win her over because she had terrible memories of cats. I found out later that she often let him sneak into her room at night and sleep with her. I shut him out of my bedroom because I'm a light sleeper, and he disturbs me. Sneaky shit. He had a mom and a mistress. That's when we dubbed him Mr. Jinx, king of the castle.

Mr. Jinx became restless in our apartment and started attacking the carpeted stairs. After attempts to dissuade him, it became apparent that the king wanted outside. It was dangerous out there, though. A busy parking lot, a forest with waiting predators, and lots of people.

What about a harness? I'd seen Jackson Galaxy on TV train cats to walk on a leash and harness, exploring their surroundings. I couldn't imagine taking Mr. Jinx for a walk, but a harness was worth a try. It would allow him to be outside.

Raised on a farm where cats ran wild, I felt foolish buying the contraption. Standing in the aisle, looking at all the choices, it seemed silly. I settled on a break-away harness designed to release the animal if it struggled hard enough. That seemed like a good idea. Finding a harness was easy compared to putting it on Mr. Jinx. He fought, and I got scratched. This was fun.

Repeated attempts and lots of patience soon landed Mr. Jinx outside our apartment, secured safely but free to enjoy the weather. Remember that fenced-in porch I mentioned? A 4-foot wood fence enclosed the porch area with a gate and cement stairs sloping toward the parking lot. I left enough length on the leash for him to roam the patio but not enough to reach the gate. At first, he struggled against the restraint and bit at the leash. He soon realized the harness meant going outside and accepted it.

After a couple of weeks, everything was going well, so I left him outside alone while I tended to household chores. When I returned, the harness was empty, dangling over the wood railing. I panicked. How had I miscalculated the distance? Did he suffer before the harness broke away? Where was my cat?

I called his name and began my frantic search. In moments of panic, the most horrible scenarios play out in your mind as you imagine the worst. What if he got run over? What if someone killed him, or he never came home? All the what-ifs made me crazy. While I was busy beating myself up, Mr. Jinx was enjoying his newfound freedom.

I spotted him two doors down, slinking under the wooden fence, a replica of ours. With a sigh of relief, I took the king home, scolding him as I went.

Turns out Jinx is Houdini in disguise, escaping every time I put him outside on his harness. When I discussed the situation with my veterinarian, she suggested letting him roam.

"This cat is pure predator, made to hunt. He'll never be happy in the house. If you allow him to go outside, it may shorten his life, but he'll have less behavior or urinary tract problems," she said.

I echoed her words in my brain. I feared losing my cat. There were so many threats out there. About the millionth time he clawed the stairs, I put him outside without a harness. Then I worried until he came home, meowing at the door. Every time I let him out, I would fret until he returned. I still do.

I know Jackson Galaxy would never approve. Perhaps you don't either, but Jinx and I understand each other.

Trying to control this cat was not possible. Whenever I think I'm in control, something reminds me I'm not. Control is an illusion. If we hold on to it too tightly, it will disappoint us when it slips away. Working with Jinx was the only solution. He was the king of this castle, and he wanted to be free to roam.

Lesson number four learned: We are not in control, especially with cats.

LESSON #5:
HOME IS WHERE YOU FEEL LOVED

We spent two and a half happy years in that apartment. They were some of the best times I had in Flagstaff. Margie was right. The perfect place had shown up.

However, Jinx and I moved again when Janella took a promotion and moved to New York. It separated our happy family forever. Janella and I sat on lawn chairs in the parking lot, drinking a glass of red wine, as we watched the movers load the boxes and furniture. This was our last night together before she was off to seek her fortune.

We reminisced, cried, and finally resigned ourselves to saying goodbye. I only had a few weeks to find a place. I guess I could've found a new roommate. Somehow that seemed like sacrilege. This had been our place. I didn't want to share it with anyone else.

Wanting to stay on the same side of town, I called a nearby room for rent. It was an enormous house, so there was plenty of space, he told me. The master suite was available, complete with a jacuzzi tub, a fireplace, and a walk-in closet the size of most people's bedrooms. It was the craziest-shaped house I'd ever seen. It looked spectacular from the outside, rising to meet the pine trees surrounding it. Two rectangular rows of windows formed a steeple in the front. Inside was a maze of rooms of all sizes and shapes. There were 5 levels, 8 bedrooms, 4 bathrooms, a half-size basketball court, a loft with a ladder staircase in the steeple, and an escape room. Designed by the owner, an architect, it was intriguing but weird. The back patio had a wet bar, a dried-up stone waterfall, 3 levels with lounge chairs scattered about, and the forest as a backdrop. I envisioned sunning myself, holding a glass of wine, and watching the sunset.

"Jinx is no problem," he said. "But there will be a pet charge of fifty dollars added every month to your rent."

"That's OK," I said happily.

He didn't tell me about the 7 other roommates, all men, until after I signed the dotted line. I hadn't asked, so I nodded, trying my best to smile. As long as I could have Jinx, the place would soon feel like home. I can always move again, I reasoned. It was a month-by-month lease, so I wasn't stuck here if it didn't work out.

Sensing my resistance, he smiled and said, "We can help you move."

Maybe having 7 male roommates wasn't so bad, I thought, pushing my inner skeptic to the back of my mind. We shook hands and agreed on Wednesday at 5 o'clock for move-in day.

They stacked my boxes outside the kitchen in the new house, which was open to the family room. There was a ping-pong table where the dining table was supposed to be. I dodged a flying white ball, followed by expletives as tempers exploded around me. Accusations flew around the room faster than the ball as I grabbed a box and rushed up the staircase to my room. This was going to be an experience. At least I could escape to my room.

I sunk into the huge jet tub, surrounded by candles, and sipped my glass of wine. Bubbles up to my chin, I relaxed for the first time in weeks. Jinx dodged the candles and padded along the narrow ledge around the tub, watching the bubbles rise. He sat on the raised platform above the tub, tail flipping, as he surveyed his new home. We had plenty of space for everything except the cat box. The only place for that was in the enclosed toilet area. Great, we could share the experience.

The daily ping-pong table battles were one of the many fun adventures at the new house. There was dirt, dust, and years of filth to deal with. The size of the house and the height of the ceilings meant it cost a fortune to heat. So, unless you want to help pay heat bills in the thousands, don't touch the thermostat. When I moved in, it was fall.

Winter seemed a long way off, and I didn't give it much thought.

I was worried about Jinx, so I kept him locked in my bedroom. There were endless ways he could get into trouble. The large house, the proximity to the forest, and seven strangers. I secretly dubbed them the seven dwarves. I was Snow White, living among the creepy little men.

There was the Asian computer geek I named Doc. He wore tiny, wire-rimmed glasses and used big words. Grumpy was easy to spot, a gym rat, meathead with a temper. Sleepy was the guy that spent most of his time passed out on the couch with the TV blaring. Bashful, the weird guy I rarely saw that hid away in his room. Sneezy was allergic to everything, ate weird food combinations, and never did his dishes. Happy was the only one I liked. He was young, handsome, and always smiling. An avid mountain biker, we hit the trails together a couple of times, but he left me eating his dust, so after the first couple of times, I passed and went alone. He moved out shortly after I moved in. Of course, the only sane one left me. Dopey was the house manager. I called him that because he walked around in a daze, pretending things were perfect, with a dopey look on his face.

I wanted to wait a week or two before allowing Jinx to explore outside my room. But when you live with other people, things don't always go as planned. Someone let

Jinx outside, and he was gone when I came home from my Saturday morning bike ride.

I spent the rest of that day searching for him while feeling sick to my stomach. I blamed my new roommates and secretly plotted revenge. How hard could it be to keep the cat inside? Why did they let my cat out? Were they trying to make me leave? All valid questions, I thought, silently fuming. This house didn't feel like home at all.

I questioned everyone, wondering who was responsible.

"Have you seen my cat?"

"Did anyone let my cat out?"

"My cat is missing. Have you seen him?"

No one in that big house cared. They didn't help or offer sympathy. Shrugged shoulders and blank looks are all I received.

Tears welled up as I sat on the dirty, carpeted stairs leading to my room. Covering my ears when the ping-ponging started. I've really lost him this time, I thought. Jinx is never coming back.

All the what-ifs I could imagine entered my brain. What if a coyote got him? What if he got lost in the forest and couldn't find his way back? What if one of my roommates did something awful to him? Tears streamed down my face. I felt lost without that dang cat. He was the only thing that made this situation livable, and now he's gone.

It was almost sunset. I peered out the enormous window that faced the forest, pouring a glass of red wine, when I noticed movement. What was that? Waving like a surrender flag back and forth. I squinted to make sure. Yep, it was the dark outline of a cat waving his tail to catch my attention.

From that moment on, I knew I was home for Mr. Jinx. He would always come back to me if he was able. This house may not be our home, but we had each other. I rushed to the door, cooing in cat tongue as the king made his entrance. I ruffled his fur, chewed him out for wandering off, and cried happy tears.

Our perfect place is out there, Mr. Jinx, and we are going to find it. This time, I didn't feel stupid for landing in a less-than-ideal living arrangement. I knew this was only a placeholder, and the perfect place was out there.

After that, I let Jinx roam the house during the day, leaving my door cracked open when I was gone. He had street smarts and an insatiable need to explore. I reminded myself that I was not in control, especially with this cat.

Nighttime was challenging for us. The only place to keep him away from my bed was the water closet where his cat box was located. I put his bed in there, giving him a comfy spot to recline, but he didn't like being confined. He was content for a few hours, but then he would howl. Jinx makes the most awful sound when he wants something. A guttural meow sounds like he's being tortured or calling a mate. It has the effect of fingernails on a chalkboard, and you just want it to stop. The more discontent he is, the louder he gets.

It's not that I minded if he was on my bed. It was my sleep challenges that dictated he slept elsewhere. I wouldn't allow him to wander my room at night, as he would jump on and off the bed, pin my legs beneath 15 pounds of catness, knead away with his claws, purr incessantly, and disturb my sleep. In the morning, I'd have bags under my eyes, feeling like the walking dead, and there wasn't enough coffee in the world to chase away my sleep deprivation.

When I couldn't stand his howling or handle one more night without sleep, I'd open my bedroom door a crack and let him wander into the house. My roommates never complained about the cat waking them, so I assumed he was quietly creeping about the castle, returning before they awoke.

The bright spot of living here was the proximity of the forest. There were trails right out the back door, leading into the trees. I could hike or bike without having to drive or load up my mountain bike. Getting my bike out of the garage was another challenge. With 8 people living in one house, there was crap stacked everywhere. We stored anything that didn't fit in our rooms in the garage. There was a bike rack, clear in the back of the garage, behind piles of stuff.

Dopey, the house manager, was a pack rat. He gathered wood pallets from around town and was using them to build a house. What? He owned land outside of town and was building a house out of the discarded pallets he picked up around town. I'd hear the guys talk about it, or he'd ask for volunteers for the weekend. I'm not sure if he paid them or not, but I never asked because I didn't care. All I wanted was to get my bike out of the garage without tripping over piles of debris, pallets stacked to the ceiling, or left strewn about on the garage floor. I've heard of houses made of a lot of different materials, but pallets? I told you this place was weird, the inhabitants even weirder.

The living situation was acceptable until the snow and cold hit. The proximity of the trails lost its allure fast as the temperature in the house dipped. There was a wood-burning stove in the family room, which helped chase away the chill when someone started a fire. It was rare, and even when one of us got a fire going, it died out quickly unless someone was feeding it.

My roommates didn't seem to be affected by the cold like I was. I walked around shivering, piling on layers until I could barely move. Jinx had long fur, which got thicker in the winter, so he never minded. I, however, suffered a great deal.

Cooking was almost impossible as my hands grew numb with cold. I spent most of my time in my room, huddled close to the portable heater I purchased in desperation. I'd move it around the apartment-sized bedroom, soaking up the heat, which never drove away the chill. This must have been what it felt like living in a castle. The walls were stone, icy, and dark; the corners were damp, and the temperature was bone-chilling inside.

To escape the cold and dreariness, I took a nightly soak in the jacuzzi tub. I'd warm the room as much as possible with the heater and run the tub with hot water and lots of bubbles. Jinx seemed to enjoy bath time. He'd walk around the tile ledge, sometimes dipping his paw in the bubbles. Then sit perched on the upper edge and watch the light from my candles dance about the room. When the jets turned on, it drowned out the ping of the little white ball, the slam of paddles, and the loud cursing. It would carry me away to some fairy tale land where the 7 dwarves did not exist.

I grew increasingly unhappy. It felt like a dungeon to me. The final straw came one night with a bang on my door. It was 2 AM. Who was there?

Bang, bang, bang! I sleep with minimal clothing, so I froze, not sure what to do. I was afraid to answer the door but afraid they might come in uninvited if I didn't. The loud banging persisted, and someone was cussing me out. It was a male voice, one of my roommates. Had Jinx woken him?

Standing in my robe behind my locked door, I screamed at the voice.

"Who is it?"

It was Grumpy.

"What do you want?" I yelled.

"Open the blankety-blank door!"

When you are the only female in a house with 7 men, you should be careful and prepared. I was both. Living in Wyoming for 30 years, and spending time far up in the mountains with the wild creatures, taught me to always have a weapon. I grabbed the black-handled knife I kept by my bedside, unlocked the blade, and stood behind the cracked door. That knife was sharp enough to lay open man or beast. I was a farm girl, a ranch hand, and a camp cook. If he was coming after me, he'd have to face the shiny steel first.

"Back down the stairs, asshole!" I screamed.

Silence.

"Get the *$#! back," I yelled.

I heard him stumble.

He was on the third step down when I opened the door enough to see him sway as he grabbed the railing. Drunk, pounding on my door in the middle of the night? This better be good.

"You're in my parking spot," he mumbled. "Move your car."

My mind raced. His parking space?

Oh yeah. It snowed heavily that day, and laws in Flagstaff required all vehicles to be off the street for snow plows. They assigned all roommates parking places. Those with the most tenure in the house got to park in the driveway, the rest of us along the street in front of the house. With the house manager's permission, I had parked in the driveway before retiring. Dopey said to park there since Grumpy wasn't home. I could move my vehicle in the morning after the snow plows passed. The message apparently never got relayed to Grumpy.

"I'll move it in the morning. Dopey told me I could park there. Now get the *$#! away from my door."

He called me a few names but stumbled down the stairs to his room.

Jinx and I spent the rest of that night cuddled on my bed. Sleep was not possible for me at this point. My hands shook as I stroked his soft fur. We both relaxed. He fell into a sound sleep, his motor running while I lay awake reading. His warm body close to mine helped my frayed nerves. I took a deep breath, rested my hand on his back, and tried to focus on the Kindle book.

The drama wasn't over yet. It had just begun. When I walked into the kitchen, Doc was getting his coffee. Everyone had their own coffee makers, espresso machines, or French presses. No one shared anything that I could tell. Not food, meals, utensils, or coffee. Every man for himself. Like a bunch of hungry lions fighting over space, claiming the right to rule. He narrowed his eyes at me, his glasses slipping onto his nose. I tried to start a conversation, despite the stress I felt.

He ignored my pleasantries and attacked.

"The nightly baths have to stop," he glared at me.

"What?"

"When you run the jets, it sounds like a freight train in our rooms. It rattles the walls and drives us all crazy."

My mouth dropped open.

The pack was circling. The only girl, the newest roommate, the easiest target.

"I had no idea," I said.

"It has to stop," he said and stomped off.

Flabbergasted, I grabbed my coffee, spilled creamer on the floor, and never wiped it up. What was one more mess on this disgusting floor?

I marched down the hall to Dopey's room. His turn to feel the wrath.

As the youngest of three, the only girl with 2 older brothers, I spent years being pushed, bullied, and picked on. It sucked growing up, but it made me tough. I was an adult woman now; I paid my rent on time every month, kept my area clean, and even did dishes others stacked in the sink for days. I swept the floor, tidied the house, and cleaned the mold growing in the refrigerator. This was the last straw. Snow White wasn't singing a merry tune by the time I reached Dopey's door.

My turn to bang on a door.

"We need to talk," I spat at Dopey. He answered in pajama pants and no shirt.

"Meet me in the kitchen. And put a shirt on," I said.

By the time he reached the kitchen, I was hissing like a wildcat. Snow White turned into the wicked witch, following him around the island, telling him of my night prowler.

"You told me I could park there. But you failed to let him know. So, he came after me. How do you think I felt, a woman alone in this house with 7 men? Someone banging on my door in the middle of the night?"

"I should be able to feel safe. You better tell that so-and-so if he ever comes near my room at night again, he won't live to talk about it!"

Then I launched into the hot-tub issue.

"You never told me about the noise it creates. Now, the guys are mad at me. I pay extra for the master bedroom and for that tub. Now, I can't use it; the one thing I actually like about this house."

He backed up a step with every word I spat until his back was against the wall.

"I feel betrayed and deceived," I said, pointing my finger in his face.

He tried to defend himself, but he knew I was right. He'd purposely withheld information to get me to move in. I later learned from one of my roommates that he was obsessed with trying to get females to live there.

He agreed to lower my monthly rent to make up for the tub. Instead of $650 a month, I'd pay $600. The others paid $550, and the additional $50 was for Jinx, which I gladly paid. And he said he would talk to Grumpy, assuring me that would not happen again. We both understood I'd be leaving as soon as I could find a place. That was my plan from the beginning. Just survive until I find a proper home. This place was so far from a home.

Two things saved me that winter. My cat and a new boyfriend that lived out of town. I escaped on the weekends to his house, the thirty-minute drive calming my nerves. He lived off the grid in the cinders. That's what they called the area on the outskirts of town that was covered in volcanic residue akin to peat gravel, dotted sparsely with ponderosa pine. The unique landscape resulted from an eruption around the year 1064. The dirt road to his house wound around stunted ponderosa and juniper bushes and through sandy crevices. I got lost many times as there were no signs once I left the pavement.

He'd spent years building the place. He heated with wood, used the wind to generate his electricity, and filled cisterns for his water. The house was simple, crafted by hand, complete with a sunroom, a yoga studio with wood floors, and a wine cellar. He hosted parties in the yoga studio. The floor was perfect for dancing. The place was so homey. Warm, inviting, isolated. An oasis in my winter world.

He offered to let Mr. Jinx come anytime I wanted. But taking the cat back and forth for weekends didn't seem right. He had settled in at the big house and enjoyed roaming the vast space. I left my bedroom door cracked when I was away so he could come and go at will. The guys let him in and out of the house when he asked, and I was no longer afraid one of them would do him harm. I had established my position; I think they knew I was no pushover. Hurt my cat; you deal with me. So, they accepted Jinx. I suspect they enjoyed having a king in the castle. They allowed him on the couch during football season and told tales of his antics when I returned after a weekend.

We didn't stay together long. Our belief systems were too different. I was a Christian; he was a Buddhist. Even though he didn't believe as I did, he recognized that two believers together would be a powerful force, so he ended things just as the weather was warming. We were both sad but resolved to forge ahead, believing life had good things for us.

I got to enjoy the love he had put into his house all those years. A love he openly shared with his friends, acquaintances, and me. That was a true home filled with warmth, generosity, and love. Board by board, piece by piece, he had labored to create a place people wanted to be. Being with him, even for a short time, gave me hope I could find a happy home.

He invited me for a steak dinner and his best bottle of wine as our last meal together. It was bittersweet. We saw each other a handful of times after that last supper. Once, when we ran into one another downtown, we passed slowly, enjoying an embrace and a kiss. He visited my place with the 7 dwarves on another occasion, returning something I forgot at his house.

Jinx and I had survived together. Against all odds, the king and I stood the test of an all-male household. It made me more determined than ever to find the right place for us. I kept telling myself this was only temporary. Surviving is no way to live, but it builds character. You get to find out what you're made of.

When I was alone in my room with Jinx, I would shut the door and close out the world. He made me happy, and I felt loved. He was my home, and I was his. As long as we were together, we would be alright, no matter where we lived.

Lesson number five learned: Home is where you feel loved.

LESSON #6:
ATTITUDE OF GRATITUDE EQUALS A HAPPY LIFE

As soon as spring came, I was hunting for new digs. I spread the word to all my friends and scoured Craigslist. It was time for something good. I put out positive vibes, believing the perfect place was out there, and it landed in my lap.

A friend mentioned he had a place for rent that would be available soon. It was located outside of town, in the forest, with two bedrooms and two baths. It was more than I could afford by myself. Time to look for another roommate.

There weren't many takers, so I accepted another guy. The house turned out to be perfect, but the roommate, not so much. He was messy, smelled bad, and was always late with his share of rent or utilities. His dog was cool, though, and got along well with Mr. Jinx. It was nice to have some muscles around the house when I needed help, so I let him stay.

There were immense pine trees in my backyard, spaced just right for my hammock when the weather warmed, fresh air galore, and a peace that filled my soul. Mr. Jinx explored with few cars or people to worry about. We found a happy home once again.

Living in the forest, there were ample mountain bike trails right out my front door. Winding through the trees, the smell of pine filling my senses was a piece of heaven.

It was time to decorate and make this house a home. I emptied the storage space that held my furniture and belongings. Things I didn't need or want were sold or donated. What fun I had unpacking boxes and finding forgotten treasures that felt like old friends. My round, bar-height kitchen table with matching chairs and wine rack fit the new house perfectly. Pictures of my kids went up on the walls, dishes I adored filled the cupboard, and outdoor furniture created a comfy gathering space for my friends. An almost new, grey leather couch and area rugs I found at the bargain store finished the look. Jinx found a favorite spot on the back of the couch. A permanent slump where he lay made me smile. Home, sweet, home.

After living in Wyoming for so long, I thought snow flew sideways. I was delighted to learn the snow in Flagstaff comes down in big, fluffy flakes that cover everything in white frosting. We had three feet at one time that winter.

Drifts so high they reached the bottom of the mailbox, sitting 3 feet up on a post. We got snowed in for one wonderful week. My car, buried under frozen drifts, wasn't moving. For a few days, the world stopped.

I felt eight years old again, walking through knee-high drifts, snow crunching under my boots, and snowflakes landing on my face. It had been that long since I'd seen snow of this magnitude. Snow that deep muffles surrounding sounds. It was a fairy-tale world or a Hallmark movie. Too good to be true. The outside world disappears, and all that is real is the surrounding whiteness. As I traipsed through the deep snow, I was grateful for the knee-high snow boots I'd brought from Wyoming, the glistening white world before me, and my new home in the trees. That winter, Jinx and I spent the evenings curled up on the couch, enjoying the warmth of the wood-burning stove, content in our cozy home.

One of the best things about living in Arizona is that the sun comes out quickly, melting away the snow. I was grateful it wasn't Wyoming, where once the ground freezes, it stays that way for almost 9 months.

On the friendship scale, my cup overfloweth. I had an amazing group of peeps. We'd met at various Meet-up groups, having arrived in Flagstaff about the same time. There was always someone up for some fun. Hiking, biking, camping, or just hanging out. We had Halloween parties, Super Bowl parties or just because parties. We used any excuse to get together. Most of my friends were younger than me, single, without children, and full of energy. Since Jinx was the only one I answered to, I took part in most of their activities. Fun was on the menu, and I ate it up. This was the life I'd wanted. The life I dreamt about while living in Wyoming was now mine. Fun, sun, and friends.

I loved living in Flagstaff. Looking back, it was one of the happiest times in my life. The feeling of being free to do what I wanted, not worrying about my kids, a spouse, or pressure to be successful, set me on a path of deep healing. Almost every weekend, I met up with my friends downtown at one of the local pubs. We'd sit for hours, sipping a hot or cold beverage, sharing a meal and our life stories. Laughter was rampant, the alcohol flowed freely, and I had more fun than I'd had in 20 years. There was live music to enjoy, outdoor patios for congregating, beer-breweries, local fare, shopping in quaint stores, and an air of peace.

A local coffee shop was a favorite gathering for Saturday morning breakfast. Cramped, dark, with old wooden chairs and tables, people piled in like sardines. The line was often out the door, standing room only by mid-morning. They roasted the coffee on the premises, so the aroma filled your senses before you walked in. This place had charm. The food was simple, with a limited menu, and the coffee packed a punch. There was nothing seemingly attractive about it, except it felt like sitting in your best friend's house, surrounded by your favorite things, drinking the best cup of coffee you ever had. We'd get there early to scavenge a table, sip our mochas or lattes, and enjoy big chunks of toasted sourdough bread slathered in butter and homemade jam. This wasn't a restaurant or a coffee shop. What they sold here was an experience.

People in Flagstaff come from all walks of life- college kids, hippies, and wayfaring strangers. There were more young than old, but no shortage of interesting characters. Bright colors, rainbows, braids, dreadlocks, beards, cool hats, you name it; you saw it. You could blend in, even if you were strange elsewhere, in Flagstaff; you were just another person in the parade of life.

I marveled at my surroundings, the place I now called home. If I'd spent 10 years searching for the perfect area to start a new life, I would never have come up with Flagstaff. It was serendipitous, and I was grateful. You could be who you truly were or wanted to be, and no one cared. You could try on a new look, style, or persona, and it didn't matter to a soul. Life was so simple. Eat, drink, and be happy. Life is good. Live long and prosper. Make love, not war. There were no pretenses to assume, no expectations thrust upon me, and no pressure to be perfect.

I could explore who or what I wanted to be. Show up dirty, sweaty, and sun-kissed after an all-day hike, slide into a booth with a funky hat, and devour pizza and beer with my hiking buddy. No one raised an eyebrow. They didn't know who I was, where I came from, what I'd done, where I'd been, or how much money I made. I was just another soul here to satisfy my hunger. Flagstaff served up fun, freedom, and fantasy. They did it so well. It was exactly what I needed.

Before I left Wyoming, I decided I would use my full name once I landed in Flagstaff. I grew up in the era where they named you one thing but called you by a shortened version or nickname. My full name was Cynthia, but everyone called me Cindy. In the past, when I tried to get people to call me Cynthia, it wouldn't last because people in a small town knew me as Cindy and refused to change. Part of my new start was to use my proper name. My brother accused me of changing my name. I didn't change my name. You people did. Humans are lazy by nature, so saying 2 syllables instead of 3 is easier. I get it. This was my chance to be Cynthia. When people would try to shorten my name and call me Cindy, I politely stopped them.

"Please, call me Cynthia."

Now, no one calls me Cindy except old friends and family. I let them get away with it because they spent so many years using my nickname, and they earned the right. But my skin crawls when someone calls me Cindy. I left her behind. She doesn't exist anymore. Cynthia is mature, experienced, and happy. Cindy was dragging around baggage, depression, and anxiety. She felt sorry for herself, took everything personally, and made bad choices. No wonder she ended up where she did. The switch to my given name gave me confidence, helping me to move forward and rise above my past. Besides, Mr. Jinx doesn't care what my name is. He's content to be with me either way.

There were only two parts of my life that didn't satisfy me. My work life and my love life.

Decent jobs in Flagstaff are scarce, especially if you need benefits. It's a tourist destination full of college students. Lots of service jobs but few solid industries. Since it's popular with outdoor enthusiasts, there is a steady flux of people moving in and out. Competition is stiff, with plenty of people that are overqualified vying for low-paying jobs with no benefits. Lots of people want to live there, but few can afford it.

When I moved to Flagstaff, I brought my job with me. It wasn't great, and it barely paid the bills, but it was low-stress. A start-up food company hired me as a marketing director for a few months before I left Wyoming. Most of my work was remote or over the phone so I was able to work anywhere. It served me well, allowing me to heal from my brush with emotional death. Despite all our efforts, the company went out of business, and I found myself unemployed for six months.

One job application after another led nowhere. I had a great resume, but I was overqualified for most of the jobs. Unemployment paid my rent, but not much more. Desperation was setting in when a friend asked if anyone in our group was interested in earning some quick cash. She was a chef at the local Elks Club. They were shorthanded for a big party on Saturday. Of course, I raised my hand!

That weekend, I stepped back into the service industry. As a young adult, I'd worked many such jobs, so it came easy. I was so grateful for the chance to earn some extra money that I worked harder than anyone else. I smiled the whole time, knowing this was temporary. At the end of the night, I had cash in my pocket. Several hundred dollars felt like I was rich. I've worked some high-end jobs, even being number 4 or 5 in a company of over 300 employees, but the satisfaction I felt that night surpassed those.

My hard work didn't go unnoticed, and they asked me to come aboard for weekend shifts, waiting tables. Three nights a week with cash tips were enough to supplement my unemployment, keeping me afloat. Working part-time hours from 4 to 11 left my days free to hike and bike the area. This was the life. It was the perfect sabbatical from the corporate world.

Waiting tables was good for a while, but what I really wanted was to try my hand at tending bar. The Elks Lodge comprised older folks. They didn't party too hard or stay up late, so the hours were reasonable. At first, I worked special events on the weekends, like banquets and weddings. I wanted a permanent spot behind the bar, not just helping with parties. My break came when one bartender got caught skimming from the cash drawer. I was the obvious choice to fill the position.

Here I was, working as a part-time bartender, still on unemployment, feeling happier than I'd been in a long time. Punching a time clock never felt so good. Every day I showed up full of gratitude. I knew it was temporary, that one day soon, I'd get a call that would put an end to my carefree life. Until then, I enjoyed every minute.

It didn't matter to me what my position was. Serving people made me happy. Pouring drinks made me happy. The more grateful I was, the happier I became. Being humbled felt amazing. I had nothing to prove to anyone. All I had to do was show up, do my job, and go home. No worries, no taking work home. Punch in, punch out. That started my attitude of gratitude. The more I was grateful for, the more grateful I became. That's when genuine happiness entered my life. For the first time in many years, I felt truly happy.

Jinx was happy in our new home. He had endless room to roam, a dog to keep him company if I was gone, and I think he sensed I was happy. Together, we were happy. Gratitude poured out of me like the drinks I served to my patrons.

Lesson number six learned: Attitude of gratitude equals a happy life.

LESSON #7:
WHAT YOU FOCUS ON EXPANDS

That dreaded phone call happened. It offered me a full-time job, ending my sabbatical from corporate life. Six months of unemployment with no health insurance was enough to make me accept the position. Even though I didn't want the job, I took it. It meant working 6 days a week in a fast-paced environment. So much for my easygoing life.

On a scale of 1-10, the job had a stress level of about 12. For a while, I freaked out, unable to handle the stress and anxiety. My job was as a salesperson for a major restaurant supply company. Racing from restaurant to restaurant, taking orders, and meeting tight deadlines with demanding, overworked chefs was not my idea of fun. Even with a good home life and supportive friends, the job was overwhelming.

When the stress became too much, my daughter, Brandie, suggested I see a yoga therapist. She and her boyfriend returned to Flagstaff after a long sabbatical and some grand adventures. She'd been studying yoga instruction and massage therapy and was on her way to receiving a degree in both. While she was taking classes, she met a therapist that specialized in therapy using yoga. I grew up in small-town Nebraska and spent thirty years in Wyoming. To say I was conservative was an understatement. Yoga therapy, are you kidding?

Brandie encouraged me, sending me the therapist's name with a phone number.

"Call her Mom," she said. "You will love her. I think she can help."

I would do about anything to keep from falling into the hole I'd just crawled out of. It was clear I was not very good at handling stress. If I had to name the character I was most like from A. A. Milne's stories of Christopher Robin, Winnie the Pooh, and the hundred-acre woods, I would be Tigger, with a little of Kanga and a dash of Rabbit thrown in. Overly energetic, worrisome, but kind-hearted most of the time. My Rabbit side fretted. My inner Tigger just wanted to have fun, often bouncing me off the walls. I needed balance.

Flagstaff is a little on the hippy side, drawing free spirits from many walks of life and offering a unique way of life. I loved it, so I say that affectionately. It was indeed a radical change from where I came from. Exactly what I needed to heal, freeing me from traditional constraints that no longer served me and stretching my thinking. I called the therapist.

We met once a week for an hour and a half in her office. I sat on the couch opposite her. First, we talked about my job, the stress, and how much I hated it. When I was all talked out, we entered a new realm.

"Are you ready to move to the floor?" she asked.

There was a natural fiber throw rug spread under the couch, covering most of the wood floor in her office. Pillows of various sizes and shapes adorned the room, available to use freely. We sat in a yoga pose (Asanas), legs crossed in front, eyes closed, while she spoke gently. I placed a pillow under my bum, tipping me forward and helping me relax.

"I want you to concentrate on your breath," she said. "Take slow, deep breaths. Focus your mind on every breath."

I was skeptical. Would focusing on my breath really help?

"Now, I want you to extend the out breath. Breath out twice as long as you breathe in."

Before I knew it, I was feeling better. I learned the out-breath was where the magic lay. That led to relaxation. Soon, I could release my breath three to four times as long as an in-breath. It wasn't large in-breaths that the body used to release tension; it was the out-breath.

Keeylan was wise. Letting me go at my pace, never pushing me into anything I wasn't comfortable with. She had the voice of an angel. I learned to meditate, relax every part of my body, and slow my heart rate. She took me on guided tours when I was ready.

I used to think there was evil in such practice that I would somehow lose myself or the ability to be in control of my mind. Nothing could be farther from the truth. A guided meditation comprised of lying in Savasana (on my back, facing the ceiling), letting my body sink into the floor, palms a little away from the hips, while she spoke gently. Sometimes I propped my feet or head with pillows or pulled a blanket across my body.

"Lift your head a couple of times to release any tight spots from the back of your neck. Now allow your eyes to close and keep them closed for the entire duration of the practice. If you feel any tension or tight spots in any part of your body, take your awareness to that body part & consciously relax that body part. It is best that you remain still during the practice, however if you become uncomfortable, please feel free to make changes with very minimal movement," she said.

Brief pause.

"It is natural to flow in and out of conscious hearing during this practice. Understand that whatever your experience is today is the experience meant for you. There is no way to do this wrong. No judgement."

Momentary pause.

"Know that you are in a safe environment & protected space. Stay awake by listening to the sound of my voice. If your mind starts wandering, which is natural, just come back to the sound of my voice."

Short pause.

"Notice any sounds you can hear in this moment, nothing else but what you can hear without straining your ears. Start by focusing on the most distant sounds. Move your attention from sound to sound without labelling the source."

Long pause.

And so it went until I was relaxed and focused on her voice and my breath. Then she would have me relax each body section, starting at the top of my head. Such practices are based on religions that went against everything I believed. But I discovered I could worship my Christian God during mediations, giving thanks and praise while allowing my body much-needed rest. Reaching a deep state of mediation meant nothing sacrilege. I was in control of my mind at all times. I could stop what was happening anytime.

The first time I went in deep during Yoga Nidra (guided meditation), I didn't even realize it until I tried to open my eyes. They didn't want to open. They felt heavy, almost glued shut. I could have forced them; instead, I allowed them to open when they wanted. My body felt heavy, slow, like a wet noodle. My inner Tigger even went to sleep.

Our sessions became my favorite part of the week. I felt better, slept sounder, and for the first time in my life, I learned how to relax my body. Keelyan recorded a Yoga Nidra session for me to play at night before I went to sleep or, if I woke up, unable to sleep. I played it until I wore the CD out.

She had me use child's pose with long out breaths in bed if I was awake for too long. Stuffing a pillow under my belly, long out-breaths, arms extended. Something about the combination is magical. I could manage my stress, anxiety, and insomnia alone if necessary. I still use this tactic and the breathing I learned when I feel overwhelmed or out of control.

Therapy helped me find relaxation and a better balance in my life, but I was missing something. My inner Tigger needed to find some fun. Enter Cynthia Saturdays.

My one day a week off became sacred, and I called it Cynthia Saturday. My rule was no work, only fun. I did nothing on Saturday that I didn't want to do. No cleaning, no cooking, no grocery shopping, just fun. It was the only way I could survive with my sanity. There were so many outdoor adventures waiting, and I planned a new one every week.

Just 30 minutes from Flagstaff through the scenic Oak Creek Canyon lies Sedona. The elevation drops from 7,000 feet above sea level to a mere 4,350. That short drive brings drastic changes in climate. It can be winter weather in Flagstaff, yet it's warm in Sedona. The grass really is greener on the other side of that canyon.

I love Flagstaff, but there is something magical about Sedona. Some say it's a mystical vortex with swirling centers of energy conducive to healing and meditation. It called to me, especially in the winter. Snow could fly in Flagstaff, yet just 30 minutes away, 400+ trails of hiking, biking, and exploring were waiting. I spent some Cynthia Saturdays enjoying both places, one adventure in the morning and a different one in the afternoon. This was an outdoor enthusiast's dream come true. It made me wonder why I spent so many miserable winters in Wyoming.

If it was too cold in Flagstaff to hike or bike, a beautiful ride down Oak Creek delivered warmth, sunshine, and endless red rock buttes to explore. If Sedona was too hot, Flagstaff welcomed me with Ponderosa pine forests, a snow-capped mountain, and proximity to the Grand Canyon.

That is what I focused on: my next adventure. It got me through stressful days at work.

I observed how Mr. Jinx spent his time. Long, blissful naps, adventurous nights, and he never missed an opportunity to snuggle. Unless there was an imminent threat, he didn't worry. He didn't fret about what would happen next or where his next meal was coming from. He had complete confidence that what he needed or wanted next would happen. And it did. My cat therapist, along with my yoga therapist, taught me how to be present. I couldn't control the world, but I could change my focus.

Whatever I thought about the most got bigger. If it was negative, all I saw was the bad. If it was positive, it got better. Big epiphany here. I have control over my thoughts. Thoughts control my actions, so if I want a happier life, I must change the way I think. This was one of the most important lessons I learned. It changed my life. Once I integrated the lesson into my mind, I put it into practice, and I still use it. When I catch myself thinking negatively about someone or some situation, I consciously stop myself.

I ask, "What are you focusing on?"

If the answer is negative, I tell myself, "Stop it."

Then I ask what is good about this. There is always something good if you look.

"Focus on that," I tell myself. Once I shift my thoughts, I find the good gets bigger, and I have more to be grateful for.

It was a shift in paradigm. A tremendous shift.

What did I want in my life? That's what I focused on. What was good in my life? Mr. Jinx, my new home, Flagstaff, my friends. At least I had a job.

Now it's easy to see that without that job, I would not have learned how to deal with stress. It was challenging, but today I am so grateful I went through it. I learned what a balanced life looks and feels like, that you can find balance in any situation once you are in control of your thoughts. I learned how to be present. Here and now, it's all we have. Worrying about the future or carrying pain from the past ruins joy in the present. By bringing things up again and again, I am harming myself with what I have already dealt with.

I often remind myself to focus on the good stuff. Let go of the bad. And then, I open myself to more good.

When I recognize stress, negative thought patterns, and harmful ways, I can step outside myself to disengage. Once I'm able to do that, I'm able to make choices toward balance. What can I control? What is outside my control? How do I take good care of myself?

Cats have a built-in balance system called the vestibular system in the inner ear and brainstem. It's how they stay balanced, giving them a sense of up and down. They can turn in mid-air, paws face down and keep their bearings. Thus, always landing on their feet. Maintaining a sense of balance is essential for survival. If something happens to a cat's vestibular system, they tilt their head, fall, roll, and lose their balance.

An unbalanced life led to severe consequences for me. In the past, when overwhelmed with stress, I would freeze up. The first thing to go was self-care. I would tell myself; *I don't have time for a soak in the tub, no time to have dinner with a friend or go for a hike ride.*

Demands of children, spouse, family, or the house came first. I put myself last for years, thinking this was a good thing. For short periods of time, it is often required in life. Long term, it becomes detrimental. And toxic.

Much like the oxygen mask dropping from the ceiling on an airplane, you must place the mask over your face first in order to help someone else. If you pass out or die due to a lack of H20, you are no good to anyone.

Giving myself permission to take good care of myself was a game changer. Instead of following a list of strict rules, like my house has to be spotless, or I can't let the laundry go, I let myself have fun. If I didn't learn to relax, find some fun, and expand my thinking, I would end up where I was before. Doing the same thing over and over, expecting different results, is insanity.

If Mr. Jinx was outside, curled up in the sun, I pulled up a chair, sipped on something yummy, and soaked in the rays. Let the dirt pile up, the dishes sit, and the laundry go. He was my teacher, and he knew how to live. When I gave myself permission to spend an entire day having fun, take advantage of small segments of time to do nothing, and luxuriate in a long conversation with a friend, things got better.

One cold, rainy Saturday, I allowed myself an entire day in bed. And I wasn't even sick. I read a good book, drank coffee in bed, and stayed in my jammies all day. Mr. Jinx beside me, the warmth of his body, the rumble of his purring, and the patter of rain lulled me into a peaceful nap. Years spent on self-imposed rules, believing the worst, and focusing on the negative landed me in the dump. Each step out of that hole took me closer to freedom, contentment, and happiness.

I may not have a built-in balance system like my cat, but there were ways to determine when I was out of sync. When I feel frozen, anxiety pulling me under, and I believe I don't have time to take a walk or a long bath, I know I'm out of balance. Once I recognize the signs, I consciously take steps to change my thoughts and behavior.

I focus on the good, let go of the bad, and check my balance. What can I do to relieve this pressure before I go over the edge? Step away from my desk, fix myself a meal or snack, and breathe. Exercise, and get some sunshine. Go find some fun!

It's having an awareness of where I am, so I can flip a switch before it's too late. I had to learn. Like a cat recognizing up from down, turning in mid-air to save itself. Mr. Jinx was not only my faithful companion but a full-time teacher. Day by day, he taught me all I needed to know for a happy life. When I catch myself focusing on problems, fears, and negativity, I turn it around in my mind and land on my feet.

Lesson number seven learned: What you focus on expands.

LESSON #8:
CATS ARE AN EXCELLENT JUDGE OF CHARACTER

It wasn't just good jobs that were scarce in Flagstaff. Good men were hard to find, too. Online dating proved interesting. I joined Match.com, put up a few pictures and a profile, and waited to see what would happen.

It wasn't long before my email inbox filled up. Every line I ever heard was used to get my attention. I scrolled through photos of men of all colors, shapes, and sizes. Well-written profiles were scarce; most were egotistical, self-focused, and exaggerated. It wasn't too hard to see through shallow, desperate men seeking sex. No… next. No… next. Maybe… I blocked the no's, sorted the maybes, and narrowed it down to yeses.

At first, it was fun. Reading profiles, scrolling through pictures. Wondering what they were like. A smorgasbord of men. Meow! The shortest date I ever had lasted 15 minutes. I saw him from across the room and knew the meeting was a mistake. He looked nothing like his picture or description. A funny little man that could barely put two words together, much less carry on a meaningful conversation. Good thing I had an escape route. A pre-planned phone call from my daughter allowed me to leave right away.

Then there was the time I faked using the restroom, knowing the back door was close enough to slip out without being seen. By his own admission, he was a deadbeat dad that abandoned his kids. That was reason enough to justify my rapid exit.

There was the incredibly hot guy I met in Sedona for a hike. Dark hair, shoulders that spanned a doorway, brown eyes, and cheekbones of a Greek god. I let him lead on the trail and enjoyed gazing at a backside you could crack an egg on. An egomaniac doesn't describe this guy. He talked down to me, spewed hatred at his ex-wife, and had nothing interesting to say. We had planned dinner after the hike. I faked a stomach issue to get out of that one. He was so self-absorbed he almost left me at the trailhead, driving off without me. The scenery was tempting, but the food was unacceptable. His good looks weren't worth his lack of taste.

Bad date after date led to more disappointment. Yeah, I was picky. I wasn't desperate, more curious than serious.

I met a few decent ones along the way. There was Rod, better known by his friends as Hot Rod since he rode motorcycles and worked on the train. If it was powerful and went fast, he liked it. On our first date, we spent over two hours talking. We laughed, drank, enjoyed each other's company, and made plans for a second date. He picked me up on his bike, handed me a helmet, and we drove into the sunset, smiling all the way. That was a good one. It lasted almost a year. I introduced him to my circle of friends, and he was an instant hit. Rod was kind-hearted with an adventurous spirit and a gift of gab. My friends became his friends.

He took me through the Wind River Canyon on his motorcycle. That was a whole new experience on the back of a bike. Wind in my face, leaning into the curves, as we wound our way down to Sedona at top speed. I could smell the clean air and hear the birds and the rush of traffic. Rod liked to go fast, and so did I. We were a good match. He was funny, made me laugh, and always had a good story to tell. Adventures on the motorcycle, parties with my friends, matching Halloween costumes, and shots of orange-flavored vodka helped me release the pain inside.

I liked to hike, camp, and mountain bike. He liked to ride motorcycles, was away 3-4 days a week on his train, and returned in need of sleep. I didn't sleep well; it drove him crazy if I was awake during the night and woke up at the crack of dawn, banging around in the kitchen way too early. He was who he was; I was who I was. The longer we were together, the less we had in common. He didn't want to hike, saw no reason to ride a bike up a mountain if you could drive up, and rarely camped. His absence and my desire to explore the out-of-doors put a great deal of distance between us. Making the 20-minute drive back and forth from his place to mine didn't seem worth the effort.

He loved Mr. Jinx and offered to let him come stay at his house anytime. Jinx liked him too, giving his purr of approval or falling asleep, stretched out on Rod's belly. But taking Mr. Jinx back and forth between our places was not what I wanted. Not for the cat, not for me, not for us, but I appreciated the offer.

My daughter, Brandie, and her boyfriend moved back to Flagstaff. She was a free-spirit, liberal-minded, and outspoken. Rod was conservative, played by the rules, and was closed-minded in certain areas. I was stuck between them, wondering why we couldn't all get along. I'm a peacemaker at heart. My new outlook on life helped me sway with the breeze, able to see both sides, not holding too fast in one direction. One holiday spent with both of them in the same house had her in tears, with him spouting off. That was the beginning of the end. Rod and I drifted apart, one weekend at a time. I would take off with Brandie and Bradley, hiking or biking a new trail. He would go off with a friend riding their motorcycles.

Brandie and Bradley knew all the secret hideaways and the off-beaten paths, and they took me along on fresh adventures. It had been a long time since my daughter and I spent quality time together. I was hungry to be in her presence, to get to know her on a new level. We went for a moonlight hike in Sedona, dinner and drinks downtown, shopping, and tea for two at a local tea room.

Brandie got Bradley into rock climbing, and together they got me to try it. First in a gym, then outside when I got the hang of it. Flagstaff has several climbing gyms, is a hub for outdoor enthusiasts, and offers rock climbers endless areas to challenge themselves. It is the only sport I have ever tried where I focused on nothing else but how to get to the next spot. The rest of the world didn't exist, only reaching the next hold.

The time she took me outside for my first climb, I discovered what trust really is. Bradley was gone for the weekend, so it was just the two of us. She was excited to show her talents and share the sport with me. I geared up, complete with a harness, climbing shoes, and a chalk bag. She showed me how to tie a knot, hold the rope and latch in. Brandie was using a Gri-gri, which is an auto-locking device for safety. Leaning into the rope (called belaying), she was taking up the slack while I inched my way up the rock. I looked down and froze. At that moment, in my mind, she held my life in her hands. If she lost focus and let the rope slip, I could fall to my death. Fear gripped tight. I screamed at her.

"You got me?"

"I got you, Mom."

"Are you sure you $*#@!ng got me?" I yelled louder.

"I got you, Mom."

"I can't make it. Let me down."

"Keep going, Mom. You can do it!"

"I can't."

"Just rest for a bit. Relax into the harness and let me hold you."

"What?"

"Let go. I got you."

"I can't let go. I'll fall."

"No, you won't. I got you; I promise."

Hanging 30 feet in the air while Brandie held me suspended was a life-changing experience. My daughter held my life in her hands. That was intense. I wasn't in charge. She was.

Once I rested and caught my breath, I resumed the climb.

Fatigue took over, and I lost confidence. *The top was too far away. I'll never make it.*

"I can't do this. Let me down."

"You aren't even trying!" she yelled.

That made me mad. I was trying.

I'll show you. Deep inside, buried for years, was the will to conquer this mountain. I just had to find it.

To make it to the top required guts, determination, and an iron will. Anything less would not get me there. I reached inside and found a renewed burst of energy fueled by anger. With determination, I grabbed each hold with purpose, pushed with my legs, and scrambled to the top. I raised my arm in victory and cried out.

"I did it!"

"I knew you could."

She knew all along how to get me to the top. Piss me off. Brandie is wise beyond her years.

I learned some people are in your life for a season. That was Rod. He entered my life when I needed him and gave me fun, friendship, and a foundation to build on. We remain friends to this day, both understanding we make better friends than lovers.

Since I had good luck finding Rod, I gave Match.com another try. I'd met him without too many bad dates, so I was optimistic. It wasn't so easy the second time around. The pool was small in Flagstaff. Most men were too young or too old. The ones my age either couldn't keep up with me on the trails, or they couldn't hold a conversation. I'd spent a good portion of my life in the gym, lifting weights and being in shape. Until the darkness entered, zapping my energy and adding pounds. With the proximity to outdoor adventure, spending my spare time hiking and biking, and eating a diet of organic food, I got back in shape fast. At 50, I was in my prime. The extra weight I gained, while depressed, fell off. I glowed. Was it too much to ask for someone in the same shape?

Young men tried to get my attention, but I wasn't interested in a fling. I wanted sustenance. Something most of them had not yet gained. It wasn't for my lack of trying to meet someone. There were plenty of one-and-done dates. Some were friendship material and great guys, but there was no chemistry for me. Others were looking only for one thing. One guy sent me a picture of "it," hoping to entice me, I guess. Delete, move on. But not before showing a couple of my friends so we could laugh together.

If a guy tried to kiss me right away, before I'd given signals, it was over before it started. They'd move in without warning, steal a kiss, leaving me shocked, not turned on. The smart ones would ask if I kissed on the first date. When the not-so-smart ones tried to kiss me without warning, I pulled away or turned my head, embarrassing them.

Kissing for me is intimate. I gotta feel it before I want to kiss you. Guys see something they like and move in for the kill. I was way past the "knock me over the head with a club and drag me to your cave" phase. Thank you very much.

Guys, if a girl is into you, you'll know it. She will touch your arm, hand, or shoulder, lean in when you talk, laugh even if your jokes aren't funny, and smile at you. She will take your arm, move close, or kiss you first if she's really into you. My advice: ask first or wait until you're sure. At least if you're over 40; otherwise, she may leave you with a mouthful of empty air or a turned cheek.

One guy walked me to my car and, after only 30 minutes together, tried to kiss me. Despite repeatedly asking me out, telling me all the reasons I should give him a chance, he informed me he only had half an hour. After a glass of wine, most of the time spent talking on the phone to his kids, he smacked me on the lips before I could stop him. I stepped back. Still, he kissed me two more times before I pushed him away. He got pissed. Me too. So long.

Communication is my love language. Quality time revved my motor. Someone I could talk to and enjoyed looking at. That was on my wish list. No wonder people give up on the dating game. It was time-consuming and frustrating.

Maybe if I expanded my reach beyond Flagstaff, I'd find that diamond in the rough. Since my job wasn't what I wanted for a career and house prices were out of my reach, I was open to leaving. The only thing keeping me in Flagstaff was an adult daughter and a love for the place. My daughter was a big reason to stay. But she had her own life, had married her boyfriend, and was busy with friends. Sure, she included me, but I felt like a third wheel. No partner of my own, no mate to go home to. Life was getting lonely. Mr. Jinx helped, but he couldn't hold me, hike with me, or help me buy a house.

It was time to look outside the box.

I called Margie.

"Picture what you want in a man. What does he look like? What does he do? See yourself holding his hand, walking beside him. What color hair does he have? How old is he?"

I tried. I wasn't very good at this.

After contemplating Margie's questions, I knew what I wanted. Adventure Man, that's who I was looking for. Someone that loved the outdoors and adventures. Someone I could have meaningful conversations with. He would be in good shape, was taller than me but under 6 foot, and have brown hair and brown eyes. That's what I put out in the universe when I expanded my search on match.com to include a 500-mile radius.

He was one of three I had narrowed down as strong possibilities. When I met him, he was smaller than I imagined and not as broad-shouldered as I wished for. On the positive side, he had a good sense of humor, could converse well, and liked to camp. By the time we met in person, we were already friends. He was an avid hiker but had never ridden a mountain bike. That would have to change. I wanted someone that would ride with me and could keep up on the trails.

We spent eight months exploring the surrounding area. He was from Albuquerque, New Mexico, and retired early, so he had plenty of time to visit me in Flagstaff. Since I worked 6 days a week, it left little time on the weekends, but we found fun on many brief adventures. Camping became a favorite, find a secluded spot, throw up a tent, light a fire, and crack open a cold beer. One good 6% IPA and I'm good, but he never seemed to find the bottom of a beer. There was always another. And he stayed stoned most of the time.

It didn't take long to figure out he was a drunk and a cheapskate. He'd bring a big cooler of beer wherever we went. When you drink more than a six-pack a day, it gets expensive, so he drank the cheap stuff and brought plenty along. After a few weekends together, I suspected he was drinking on the trip from Albuquerque to Flagstaff, but I'd be so happy to see him that I let the smell of beer go without mention.

My company hosted an enormous party in Phoenix one weekend. I took him as my guest. They put us up in a 5-star hotel and provided meals, beverages, and entertainment. Still, he carted that cooler up three flights of stairs in front of my co-workers. Embarrassed, I covered for him, making up some story about what was in there.

To be fair, there was also food in the cooler. He liked to eat the same thing every day and didn't enjoy going out. The only meal my company didn't provide for both of us that weekend was breakfast on our departing day. I suggested a nearby restaurant. There was nothing for me to eat in the cooler, and we would travel several hours back to Flagstaff. I drove my vehicle to Phoenix, paid for the gas, and my company provided everything else. When the check came, he hesitated and looked at me.

Are you kidding?

"I think you can take care of this one, right?" I said.

"I guess so," he said, slowly picking up the check.

My gut felt tight, and I swallowed hard, but I let it go.

I never spoke up. I covered for him, lied to myself, and allowed his behavior to continue unchecked. When we visited friends or family, he brought along a hand-held cooler. He made sure he was never without a cold brew. I played the familiar role of co-dependent, never asking if he was drinking while driving to Flagstaff. In my heart, I already knew, but I ignored it. When he became paranoid or forgot details, I laughed it off. I allowed him to do as he wished, not wanting to upset the apple cart. That was on me.

I liked to go downtown in Flagstaff, sit outside, and have a beer on an outdoor patio or eat out once in a while. He didn't enjoy going out or the Flagstaff atmosphere. However, he was happy for me to provide his meals instead of eating out of his cooler. I cooked; he ate. We would run to the grocery store before camping, stock up on what we needed for the weekend, and I would pay. After a few weekends, I asked if maybe he would cover the groceries this once. That was the only time I remember him paying for food at the grocery store that we both consumed. I justified it since he drove to Flagstaff regularly. I went to Albuquerque only a few times. Of course, he was retired, and I was working 6 days a week.

Red flags were flying all over. I should have confronted him, but I wanted to ride it out. After all, I was having fun. That's how I justified things. I was tired of dating; trying to find a mate was hard. So, I settled.

We reached the decision point in our relationship. Time to take it to the next step or move on. We decided I would move to New Mexico. The weather was favorable for my SAD. The job pool was much bigger, and he owned a house with plenty of space. Leaving Flagstaff was hard. It was my happy place. My daughter was pregnant with her first child, so it wasn't a simple decision. I would miss out on so much. I'd applied for many jobs, trying to stay. Selling timeshares in Sedona was an option but not one I took seriously. It felt too scammy, and I just couldn't get myself to do it. Reason overruled my desire to stay. I hated my job and needed more sunshine, and if this didn't work out, there were more dating opportunities in Albuquerque.

My daughter took it hard. My heart broke for both of us. This isn't what I wanted. There just wasn't a viable future in Flagstaff for me. I could have asked Adventure Man to move my way. He might have been willing. He loved the area and asked around for prices. Houses weren't out of his price range, just mine. That did not solve my job issue or the need for more sunshine and warmer weather.

I had eight wonderful months in my new home. Outside of my roommate, this had been my perfect space. Fear of such a big change, leaving my daughter, and an uncertain future haunted me. Would Mr. Jinx adapt? How would he deal with city life? We both loved this house and the area. I fretted, questioning my decision. There was no way to know if I was doing the right thing until I was there.

I can always move back. It's only a few hours away. I can come to visit my daughter and grandchild often. This isn't final. I can always change my mind.

My roommate was a poor decision I'd made and had to deal with before moving to Albuquerque. He owed me back rent and utility money, falling further behind every month. I was the one that allowed him to move in. I let him slide on the deposit instead of holding out for someone that had money in hand. Now, I was paying the price.

I left notes on a magnetic board attached to the fridge, as we didn't see each other much. Sometimes the money would show up, stuck to the fridge under a magnet, but most of the time, it didn't show at all. I knew I was moving out in a month, so I gave notice to my landlord and left a letter for my roommate, asking for the balance he owed.

What I received was an obvious message. He had stabbed through the board with a knife; the letter was gone, the damaged board his reply.

Shaking, I called Adventure Man. We decided the money was not worth the risk of a crazy roommate doing me harm. He had to leave my house fast. So, I lied. I told him I had to be out sooner than expected, and if he could be out by the weekend, I would forget about the money he owed.

Money is an excellent motivator, especially when you don't have any. He was out in two days. Goodbye and good riddance. Hopefully, that was the end of crazy roommates.

What happened next should have been a clue that there were more opportunities for me to learn that bad choices have negative consequences. The night before we were to leave for Albuquerque, all but the last of my things loaded in the U-Haul truck, I realized my car keys were missing. I always put them in the same place, in the brown bowl on the counter. Somehow, they got misplaced. We searched everywhere, except all the boxes stacked at the front of the truck, heavy furniture blocking our way. The plan was that he would drive the U-Haul, and I would drive my vehicle. It's hard to drive without keys.

My vehicle was a Nissan with a coded key fob and had to be towed to the dealer. A phone call to a friend (thanks, Roger) who owned a towing business saved the day. $700, and hours later, we headed for Albuquerque. Of course, I racked my brain trying to figure out what in the world happened to my keys. I had never lost my keys. I paid the whole thing out of my pocket with money I didn't have. Never once did Adventure Man offer to help until days later when I asked if he would pay half since it wasn't clear who was responsible.

About a year later, I found those keys. In a pocket on my Camelbak (backpack with drinking water system). A place I'm sure I never placed them.

Jinx and I drove down the road together, headed to a new future. He was in the crate riding shotgun, just like old times. My daughter had packed me lunch for the road. Her choice of goodies delighted me. She didn't come to help me pack or load the truck. I think my leaving was too hard for her. She showed up just as we were pulling out of the driveway, handing me a brown bag. She expressed her feelings when she handed me my lunch. My daughter created finger food out of all my favorites, figs, nuts, an apple, and dark chocolate, that was easy to eat while driving. There was love in that bag. I was going to miss her so much.

Adventure Man and I never would've made it a year without our spoken agreement. A promise between us, sealed with a shot. No matter what, we agreed to stay together for one year. First, I was tired of moving. Second, I knew it was going to take me at least a year to adjust to a new town, a new job, and a new living arrangement.

Statistically, that raised my stress level pretty high. So, I'm the one that insisted on the one-year contract.

What I didn't face was that I gave up my power when I moved in with him instead of getting myself a place. I was afraid to live alone in Albuquerque. My bank account was long ago drained of savings, making it hard to come up with a deposit and two months' advance rent. I wanted stability and a break from trying to make it alone. All good points, but moving in with him led to more dependence instead of independence. Then there were his addictions, which I never confronted. Instead, I turned a blind eye, accepting it without complaint.

When you live with an addict, there is a certain amount of chaos swirling around, waiting to upset your world, like misplaced items, broken promises, and missing keys. The mishap in Flagstaff wasn't the last time keys went missing. There was the weekend we visited my daughter, Calli, in Colorado, and he locked the keys inside the trunk before I could stop him. There was no mistaking who did what this time. Being high apparently causes impairment in judgment. Then you have to ask your daughter to drive you to the local car dealership and spend most of your weekend getaway waiting for a new key.

Addicts rarely take responsibility for their actions or realize the depth of the damage they cause. Little by little, trust dwindles away. The greater the addiction, the greater the chaos. The other thing about addicts is their affections are for that one thing. That is their true love. They spend their time, money, and effort chasing after the next fix. That's how the next few years went.

He lived in a big house on the hill, one he was very proud of. In reality, it was outdated and in need of upgrades. Every wall was the same boring beige. I hated it, and he wouldn't let me change a thing. It was like living in an old museum. Relics of a past life stacked in closed-off rooms, covered in dust.

Adventure man owed nothing on the house. He had paid it off years earlier, but still, I forked over $500 a month in rent. Over 3 years, that added up to more than $18,000 I put in his pocket. Deep down, I hoped if we broke up that he might have been saving some of it to give back and help me get a new start. That never happened. Adventure Man was stingy. My part in the dysfunction was expecting things to be different while not taking a stand. Hoping he would marry me, wanting someone to save me.

We didn't go out very often, and he rarely paid for anything we did together. That's why he had money, I guess, but it was very unattractive. If we took a trip, we would split the costs. I paid my way, not wanting to feel I owed him anything. Until the day he asked me to pay for half of the toilet paper. There were three bathrooms in the big house. I only used one, and I purchased my own toiletries. I laughed. Not doing that, sorry, Stingy Man.

He reminded me often it was his house. When he blew up one day, asking why I didn't help with the yard work or upkeep on the house, I reminded him; it was his house. I was just a renter. Smile.

Jinx wasn't happy either. The uppity neighborhood was full of new threats. The biggest nuisance lived in our house and tormented him. A spoiled sheltie dog that took every opportunity to chase or chastise Mr. Jinx. Though I loved the dog, I grew tired of the owner (my boyfriend), who allowed such behavior to go unchecked. Of course, Mr. Jinx could have set the dog straight. He was a top predator, equipped with razor-sharp claws and long fangs. Jinx doesn't fight dogs, sometimes to his demise. His mode of behavior is to slink away or remain still. It has served him well in certain situations, but not with this menace.

Then there were the neighborhood bullies. Pound for pound, Jinx should be a badass cat. Weighing in at almost 14 pounds, with long, thick fur for protection, you would think he would be the one kicking butts. He's an outstanding hunter with street smarts, but his fighting skills are lacking. I spent over a thousand dollars patching him up after many scraps left him injured. The most serious fight almost cost me my cat.

He disappeared for several days. When he came home, it was apparent he needed another trip to the vet. This time it was going to cost me $1,600, money I didn't have. Something or someone had dragged my poor kitty along the pavement, resulting in torn front paws and a broken canine tooth in his upper jaw. Surgery to remove the broken tooth was required.

With tears in my eyes, I told the receptionist I didn't have that kind of money. Either they cut me a deal, or my precious kitty would have to be put to sleep. They wouldn't budge on the price. My companion was no help. He had plenty of money but never offered a dime. The situation revealed his true character, making me feel worse.

I sat in the waiting room alone, tears streaming down my face as I readied myself to say goodbye to Mr. Jinx.

When the doctor was out of sight, the receptionist asked me to come to the desk. She handed me a piece of scrap paper with a name and number written.

"Here is the name of another place you might try. I don't want to see you have to put Mr. Jinx down. I think they'll do the surgery for much less."

God bless that girl. She risked her job to tell me there might be a way to save my cat. When you live in a ritzy part of town, I guess they get to charge more. You will be happy to know that Mr. Jinx recovered. He has a funny smile now. When they removed the canine tooth, it left him with a droopy upper lip that gives him a comical look. There must be a special place in heaven for people like that receptionist. I will always be grateful to her.

Did I mention the man I lived with not only didn't like cats but was also allergic to them? Or so he said. I never witnessed sneezing, wheezing, or signs of an allergy. Stingy Man ignored Jinx most of the time. Rooms were closed off, including the master bedroom. He built a special door with wire mesh to allow cool air to flow in the master bedroom while keeping the cat out. Mr. Jinx must have felt the hostility because he soon got revenge.

A dog door allowed both animals to come and go at will. Jinx learned how to navigate the plastic flap that separated the outside from the inside. At first, I wasn't sure if the "gifts" he brought into the house were peace offerings or antagonistic tools. Dead or alive, the prizes were not welcome. I would arrive home from work to some new catastrophe. Bird feathers strewn about, dried blood on the carpet, and an angry partner. The live mouse proved to be the most fun. Two adults chasing a tiny mouse through an enormous house must have been entertaining to my cat. He sat watching, licking a paw, rubbing it over his ears.

We set traps all over the house in case another live varmint got loose. Adventure Man was obsessed with checking the traps, although they were always empty. I couldn't stop Jinx from bringing in unwanted pets. As long as the dog door was open, the cat continued his behavior. Fights became frequent between us. I suspected he and the cat were fighting while I was away. I hoped he wasn't hurting the cat, but I never really knew what transpired between them during the day.

Not that I thought Stingy Man was evil, just that he was so frustrated with the cat by the time I got home. I was certain he manhandled him because Mr. Jinx did not approach him or try to jump on his lap. The cat avoided his space, his chair, and kept his distance. That was a sign. Jinx likes most people and will often approach visitors, quickly making friends. Even jumping up uninvited, hoping to get a good petting. Stingy Man often commented he wished I didn't have a cat and that he wouldn't allow another one in the future.

He owned land in the mountains, passed down from his parents, on which he planned to rebuild a cabin that burned in a forest fire. Summer weekends found us riding his four-wheeler, sleeping beneath the stars, and clearing brush from his plot. I worked side-by-side with him in the scorching sun and slept on the cold ground or a dirty, old mattress at his uncle's cabin without complaint. Building his future. Somehow, I imagined I would be part of it.

The outdoors called to me, and this reminded me of my years in Wyoming. A mountain getaway seemed worth the sacrifice of my weekends, driving several hours one way, bone tired when we returned on Sunday evening. While I went to work on Monday, he slept in, lounged in his hot tub, and drank the coffee that I made for him. Such a lucky girl.

After two years, I assessed the situation. By now, I was over the culture shock of moving to Albuquerque. I was working at a contemporary furniture store, using my creative side for the first time in a while. I loved helping people design their homes. It was the first job I'd had in years that I found fulfilling. The problem was it was a straight commission. It took a year before I was making a decent living. Every month I stressed over sales. In New Mexico, I was making a living wage, but it was far from my previous corporate job. There was enough to pay my bills but not much for savings.

I was afraid to live alone in Albuquerque. The crime rate is pretty high. I was a small-town girl in a big city, and I wasn't street-smart. Life on the hill sheltered me from that part. It was comfortable here, even if less than ideal. I stayed for another year. They say at the two-year mark in a relationship, you have a good idea of what the other person is like. Before that, most of what you see is a masquerade. Each portrays the best part of themselves. It's too hard to keep the pretense going much longer than two years so I knew what I was getting. A drunk, a stoner, and a cheapskate.

Still, I longed for him to love me. I loved him and told him often. Those three words left his mouth two times in three years. It's easier to connect the dots looking back than when you are in the situation. The motivation I needed to move on was not yet bigger than my fear of leaving or my desire to be loved.

I was in Peter Pan mode. Wanting to be carefree and have fun. Here, I got to pretend I was the princess living in the castle. Dreaming, the handsome prince would confess his love and sweep me off my feet. Instead, he ran off with his lost boys. Taking extended trips to Alaska and Colorado, fishing, or working on his cabin, leaving me alone in the castle.

A turning point came when I got sick with bronchitis. I missed two full weeks of work, had a fever so high I lost my taste buds, and drug myself to the doctor just in time to prevent pneumonia. Sicker than I have ever been, he left me to suffer alone. I spent sleepless nights on the couch, propped up on pillows, having coughing fits that exhausted me completely. Not once did he tend to me, bring me a meal, or offer help. The fairy tale life was no fun, and we were not living happily ever after.

At the three-year mark, I knew it was time to move on. No long-term commitment was coming, he assured me. He felt trapped and unhappy. I had to stop fooling myself that things would be different. Being here had given me stability and more time to heal. We had a lot of fun along the way, despite the challenges. I stayed as long as I did because I was still playing Peter Pan, running from responsibility. It was time to step up and own my life.

Unbeknownst to him, I had been investigating how I could buy a house using my retirement accounts. I saved enough along the way for a down payment on a house. He laughed when I told him my plan and made a joke about a fixer-upper being the only thing I could afford. Surely, I would need his help to get any place I could afford livable. When someone tells me I can't do something, it makes me want to do it even more, especially when they make fun of me. Thank you, Stingy Man; just what I needed for motivation.

After looking at two dumps, my realtor asked if I'd seen the last property she emailed. The price was higher than I'd budgeted, but she wondered if I might like to see it. When I pulled into the driveway, I knew this was my new home. The house was cozy, with two bedrooms, two full baths, mature landscaping, and a fenced-in backyard. It had everything I wanted, including a garage for me and a cat door for Jinx. Seven years had passed since we left Wyoming. Wandering around like nomads, finding fun, sun, and adventure, it was time for a place of our own. The offer got accepted. Jinx and I were ready to put down some roots.

The constant harassment, the long recovery from surgery, and time had taken its toll; Mr. Jinx was failing. He'd lost weight, was lethargic, and I wasn't sure he would survive one more move. Worried the change would be too much, I contemplated putting him down. My life would never be the same without my cat. We had come so far together. Would fate allow us the chance to enjoy a home of our own?

Good thing I waited. Jinx soon thrived at the new house. He had a new neighborhood to explore, a fenced-in yard for security, and a large picture window with a view. There weren't many tough cats in the area, making him king. I surmised his weight loss and lethargy were because of depression. I didn't know cats got depressed.

The vet bills stopped. Jinx gained weight. I had the walls painted in cheerful colors. No varmints, dead or alive, showed up in the new house. Life was good for the king and me. It became apparent the animals he'd brought to Stingy Man were his way of saying he didn't like him. Jinx had been trying to tell me he wasn't happy, that this guy was not the one. Had I listened to my cat early on, when we first met Adventure Man, it could have saved me another *opportunity* to learn a hard lesson.

I called Margie.

"Cats always know," she said. As an owner of multiple cats herself, she was well aware of their keen sense of people.

"Were there signs early on?" she asked.

"Yes," I admitted.

"Well, now you know. This is just another opportunity to learn."

"I'm tired of *opportunities*. When will they stop?"

"When you have learned the lesson," she said.

From now on, anyone I let get close to me had to pass the Mr. Jinx test of approval.

Lesson number eight learned: Cats are an excellent judge of character.

LESSON #9:
HAPPY IS AS HAPPY DOES

If life was so great in my new house, why was I on the floor with a glass of wine each night, crying over my lost love?

Because I was feeling sorry for myself. The way I had every time a relationship ended. Woe is me. That was what I did. Relive all the disappointment, wallow in self-pity, and blame him for not being a better man, not taking responsibility for my part.

Mr. Jinx rubbed against me as if brushing me with his happiness. It took so little to make him happy. But then, he was a cat. What if I could be like that? Just be happy because I could.

The radio was playing a song I'd never heard… one line sunk in. Happy is as happy does. The message was clear: if you do things that make you happy, you will be happy. The choice was mine. I wrote it on the refrigerator magnet in big, bold letters. I had been doing things that made me happy, but I was still allowing things to happen to me, keeping quiet when I should speak up, and being reactive instead of proactive. For the past 8 years, I had been in Peter Pan mode, having fun, shirking responsibility, and living like a nomad. That was OK. I needed that time to heal. Now was a new phase. A time to lay a solid foundation for the future. Create a new paradigm.

If I wanted a different life, I had to make different choices, look ahead at what I wanted, and make a plan to get there. Things, people, and places added to my happiness, but they didn't produce it or sustain it. That must come from me. It was time I learned to carry happiness with me wherever I went. Put it on every day, like my clothes or makeup. Do happy, be happy.

I realized I could still be happy, even if things went sour. Instead of focusing on the hurt, I shifted my focus to all the good things in my life. There was a lot of good. Here I was, in my home. A house I bought, a place that was charming, and everything I could ask for, with Jinx by my side. This was a brand-new start. I'd waited all these years to have a place to call my own. No crazy roommates to deal with. I could decorate, create, do what I wanted with the house, and no one could stop me.

I got up off the floor, wiped my tears, and took control of my life.

What made me happy? Hiking, riding my mountain bike, being with friends, enjoying good food, and feeling loved. Good, do those things.

What didn't make me happy? My job. I'd quit the furniture store and went to work for a local flooring outfit. Living on straight commission was too stressful, and I was tired of working retail with forced holidays and weekends.

I was optimistic this time. The owner of the flooring store made big promises for new accounts and more money to get me to take the job. Promises that were never fulfilled after several years. He had a keen way of making people feel stupid. Talking down to us, using shame and blame on anyone that didn't learn the flooring business as fast as he thought they should. There was a lot to learn, but since I was in Peter Pan mode, I just laughed it off. I liked the work and got to decorate entire houses for people, so I kept hoping things would get better, just like I did with Stingy Man. It didn't get better. Had I learned nothing? I stopped laughing. It wasn't funny. I was wasting my time and talent.

It was time to find a new job and a new man.

Within two weeks, I met a good man on match.com. Time was wasting, and I wasn't getting any younger. Either I stay in self-pity, or I move on. Every time thoughts of sorrow, pain, or misery from my failed relationship entered my mind, I stopped them. I focused on the good things instead.

Stop it! Quit feeling sorry for yourself. Focus on all the good things.

Was it that simple? Yes, and no. It was a process. When negative thoughts entered my mind, I stopped them and switched to positive thoughts. Even if it was the smallest thing, I became grateful for it. The smell of coffee in the morning, sunlight on my face, dark chocolate, a sunset. Mr. Jinx's antics. The more I did, the happier I felt.

The better I felt, the easier it was to make good decisions. One excellent decision led to another. One poor decision wasn't the end of the world. Misery was of my making, in my head, reliving the details. When it's over, it's over. Deal with it, then move on. The only power the past had over me was what I gave it. Epiphany!

I also learned to sit with my pain, observe it, and even lean into it without allowing it to drown me. Sit in it for a time, or let it wash over me. The decision was mine. I had better things to do, so the choice was easy. Instead of running from pain, avoiding it at all costs, I learned to control how long it hung around. Emotional pain is of our own making. Sure, painful things happen, but it's remembering and focusing on that pain, reliving it repeatedly, that keeps us in pain.

That's the major lesson I gleaned from Byron Katie in the book Loving What Is. There are four questions you ask yourself to do what she refers to as The Work. Once I learned to apply the questions, it freed me to be happy.

I could choose to keep reliving painful experiences, or I could let them go. Either way, it happened. The difference is, will I allow it to ruin my day, my night, and my life? Is there any good reason to keep reliving this?

I know now that I stayed with Stingy Man for three years because I wasn't ready to move on. Fear stopped me. My beliefs held me back, thinking things would get better. He would come to his senses and realize he loved me. Feeling I would be whole only if he married me. Connecting the dots after looking back is easy. When I was ready, I moved on. Until then, I was where I was. It gave me time to gain perspective.

Margie helped me see my part.

"Ask yourself two questions. What is my part? What could I have done better?"

Taking responsibility, instead of casting blame, was a big lesson. One I needed. She held up a mirror for me. That is genuine friendship. Telling someone the truth instead of what they want to hear. She does that a lot. It's not always easy to hear, but it sure helps me grow.

My creative side blossomed, working as a designer, reigniting passion within me, and taking me closer to who I was under all that pain. During my solitude, my imagination burst forth.

Positioned on the floor with a large chalkboard to fill, hands covered in colored powder, I found my inner child. A part of me that lay hidden for years came alive in brilliant colors. Elephants, cats, birds, whatever struck my fancy. The pictures were temporary creations, allowing me to erase them and begin with a fresh idea. I didn't have to finish the piece; I could just wipe it away on a whim. I was free to choose. Happiness welled up inside of me, spilling over into creativity and healing my soul.

It might have taken much longer to revive my creativity if it hadn't been for being alone. That is how you practice gratitude. Find the good and focus on that.

First, it was art, then homemade cards. Finally, I wrote. When I was growing up, I was an avid reader, devouring books like a starved child. I dreamed of becoming an author. Through the years, I penned stories, poems, and even a children's book, but at some point, my creativity left, taking my dreams of being an author with it. That part of me packed away like an old suitcase sitting in the closet.

I did not waste those years with Stingy Man. In fact, I see them as a gift. Each step took me closer to where I am now. Stronger, smarter, more confident. My breakdown left me broken and diminished. Recovery took much longer than I imagined. What I learned is there is no time limit for healing. It takes as long as it takes. Without the trials, the hard knocks, and the long process back, I would not have written this book. As hard as those lessons were, they released pain I didn't even know I was holding. My Peter Pan mode put me back in touch with my fun side. It did little for my career or bank account, but it was a necessary part of recovery. I had tied poor Tigger down for too long. Once I set him free, he bounced higher than he ever.

The guy on match.com? Turns out I attracted something good this time. Our first date was uneventful. We met at Olive Garden for dinner after talking on the phone a few times. He wore a black cowboy hat and talked like a hillbilly, but he was kind, so I gave him a chance. A brief hug between us, enough for me to know he smelled good, was encouraging. He held the door and told me I looked very beautiful as the hostess led us to a booth. There was no two-hour-long conversation. The date was short but long enough for me to know I wanted a second one.

He ate fast and talked enough for me to know he was intelligent, even with his dialect. He worked with computers as a cyber-security agent for the government. Really? It was a story you weren't sure was real. He didn't look like a computer guy; he looked like a cowboy. The hat and the goatee were deceiving. Underneath was an intelligent and direct man.

"Do you kiss on the first date?" he asked.

I swallowed hard, then smiled. "No."

"Ok. But just know I'm thinking about it."

Now that was sexy. Smart guy, good start.

This guy didn't mince words. It was clear he said what he meant and meant what he said. We flirted over text the next few days, talked on the phone, and got to know each other. He was funny and made me laugh. He'd been in the Coast Guard, played video games, and went country dancing every weekend. That was an interesting combination. When he asked me out for Friday night, of course, I said yes. We met at the country bar where he was a regular. Black cowboy hat, hooded brown eyes, friendly smile. I found him very attractive. I hadn't seen many men in cowboy hats since I left Wyoming. You can take the girl out of Wyoming, but you can't take Wyoming out of the girl.

He met me at the door, paid my way, took my hand, and led me to his favorite table. Then he smiled, leaned over, and stole a kiss. I kissed back. He'd honored my first-date rule, but it was clear he wasn't waiting until the end of the night for a kiss.

I was nervous about dancing. He was a regular here. I didn't know who was who and hadn't danced country since I left Wyoming. We walked onto the floor for a two-step.

"Just relax," he said. "Anything that goes wrong out here is my fault."

Big smile on my face as we moved around the floor. I was awkward; he was patient. We both enjoyed ourselves and kissed more. That second date led to another and another. We each closed our match.com accounts and dated exclusively.

A few months after I bought my house, Stingy Man came to see me at work. He looked sober, dressed sharply in clothes I had helped him pick out, and asked if he could talk to me for a few minutes. We walked in silence to the back of the store for privacy.

I stood, stunned, while he cried, confessing he loved me. He couldn't get me out of his mind. Would I give him another chance?

Empathy was what I felt, not love. Too little too late, mister. I'm with a good man now. We hugged, him holding tighter and longer than I did. He walked away, holding his head down. I smiled to myself. I made the right choice. Mr. Jinx would be glad to hear we weren't going back to the big house. He was happy in our abode, and he was thriving again.

When I got home, I told Mr. Jinx the entire story as he peered out the front window, lounging on his throne up high. He looked at me, eyes half open, and grinned with his toothless crooked smile.

Lesson number nine learned: Happy is as happy does.

LESSON #10:
TWO ARE BETTER THAN ONE

When I moved into my new home, I adopted a dog. Mulan was a Rhodesian Ridgeback shepherd mix. Beautiful, smart, and needed a patient owner to handle her aggression toward strangers. Either she suffered trauma or lacked proper socialization as a puppy because she had issues. She had been in and out of foster homes, obedience trained through a prison program, feared strangers, and hated men.

Ever since leaving Wyoming, I wanted to get another dog. The time was not right until now. I needed to feel safe at home, out hiking, or going for a walk. She was protective, mostly out of fear, but she fit the bill. Over the years, I had trained many dogs, so I was confident I could handle her. We both needed each other.

When I met her for the first time, she snarled and barked at me. I was nervous, but it only took a few minutes for her to relax, lying at my feet, chewing on a toy. She was in a foster home with several other dogs. The place was too small for the inhabitants. Two adults, three foster kids, large dog crates, and a tiny backyard. We went for a walk and I discovered the depth of her fear. A garage door opened, and she bolted, almost breaking free. Then she tried to wrestle out of her collar, whining and fighting with me. I got us back to the house, heart pounding, Mulan dragging me. She was going to take more work than I thought, but I was up for it and signed the adoption papers.

Our first night alone was a memorable experience. She didn't yet trust me. She was crate trained, which saved the day. *Thank you, foster parents.* It served as a safe space for her, allowing me to leave without worrying my house would be in shambles upon my return. And I didn't know how she would react to Mr. Jinx. I was still moving my stuff and had to make a last trip, leaving her alone for a short time. It was dark when I returned home. I passed the crate to turn on the lights, and a deep growl came from inside. Great, I'm alone with a dog that wants to eat me! This was my dog now. There was no one but me to take care of her; we had to figure this out. Luckily, she was food motivated. Treats tossed into her crate, a sugary sweet voice, and slow movements allowed me to open the crate without getting bit.

Mr. Jinx proved his superiority when I introduced the pair. I had Mulan on a leash, Mr. Jinx lounging on the bed when she noticed him. Maybe she had never met a cat face-to-face before. Fear took over, escalating the situation from aggressive to dangerous in a flash. Mulan was in attack mode, snarling and barking in Mr. Jinx's face before I could stop her.

If that cat had moved before I got a tight grip on the leash, Mr. Jinx might not be here. He sat still, faced with danger, unwavering. Good thing he didn't take fight or flight. It took weeks to train Mulan to accept the cat. Every time she didn't respond to him, she got a treat. The slightest improvement landed her a tasty reward. Soon, the two pets could be together in the same room alone, without my intervention.

Mulan slept on her bed in my room. Jinx locked out at night (sorry, but he disturbs my sleep). He got his revenge during the day, taking over her comfy spot. Mulan would whine, circle the cat and bark. He ignored her, staking his claim.

I knew when I found them curled together on Mulan's bed; we were a family. When I wasn't looking, the dog chased the cat; the cat teased the dog in equal measure, but they were friends.

Our new happy place was the back porch. A glass of wine, a comfy chair, Mr. Jinx asleep under the honeysuckle bushes, and Mulan curled at my feet. Same red wine I drank on the floor, feeling sorry for myself, but a very different outcome. I had the best of both worlds. A cat and a dog to love. Life had come full circle, with a home, two pets, and a happy heart.

Mulan accepted Jinx quickly, but it took longer for her to trust the man in my life. She made it clear she didn't like men. Maybe she suffered under a rough one or knew only female owners. Either way, it took my boyfriend, Brian, at least 6 weeks to win her over. He would sit beside her crate, talking to her, feeding treats through the opening in the side. She snarled and snapped but ate the treats gladly.

If we were hiking and she spotted a man in the distance, she would growl, hair standing on end like a porcupine. Rhodesian Ridgebacks have a line of hair along their shoulders that stands tall when provoked. If the man headed in our direction, she would fight and wrestle to get loose. I desensitized her to men the same way I did to my cat, rewarding her for *not* reacting. At first, we would turn and walk in the other direction if there was a man headed our way. She needed to trust that I would not put her in a situation she could not handle. When she relaxed, in the slightest, she got a treat.

We progressed to turning away if a man approached, getting off the trailway with treats forthcoming to distract her. Soon we could pass a man without a blowup. She would be nervous but remained at my side without bolting. Despite our training, now and again, she reacted aggressively, but it was rare.

Brian became her favorite person. He played with her, brought her treats, and she went berserk when he showed up at my door. The first time he took her for a walk without me, she escaped, racing home, leash dragging behind. After about a year, she trusted him as much as she trusted me.

Mr. Jinx loved Brian. The two of them would lounge in a chair, Mulan beside them, while we watched our favorite shows. Part of me felt betrayed by my pets, and the other part was delighted they took to him. I trusted their judgment over my own.

Still working at the flooring store, I was increasingly unhappy. I was actively searching job sites, sending resumes, and turning down offers. This time, I wasn't looking for another *opportunity* to learn a hard lesson. I was searching for the right place to land. All the best jobs I saw were in insurance, offering top benefits, high pay, best sales opportunities. Thoughts of my experience in Wyoming flooded over me. I shuddered at the idea of going back to the insurance industry.

Then Covid hit, and it forced most of us to work from home, or we lost our jobs. My company sent us to work remotely for 3 months. The world changed. Life changed; jobs either evolved or went away. I enjoyed the time spent in my home, being able to walk to my desk instead of driving 25 minutes across town in traffic. I was more relaxed and more productive, without endless interruptions at the store. Mr. Jinx loved it too. He'd curl up on my chair if I left it for a few minutes, lay on the floor beside me, or crash on his bed in the corner. As a co-worker, he was a slacker, but being around him, all day was soothing. They asked me to return to work at the store, but wearing masks drove me crazy. My glasses fogged up. It was hard to breathe. The drive to and from my job now felt tiresome. I had a taste of working remotely and decided that would be my future.

Brian worked out of his home and had for years. That's what I wanted, to work remotely in a career that was Covid proof, at a job that I could do from anywhere. What if we wanted to move or go on an extended visit? Remote work for both of us was the answer. That became my top priority. I was getting a clear picture of what I wanted.

A series of bad bosses, poor managers, and lousy pay left me hungry to find where I belonged. It had to be out there. My dream was to be rewarded for hard work and dedication. To be paid for what I was worth. A company that would offer over two weeks off a year. Brian had so much vacation time he didn't use it all. I wanted to find out what that felt like. He had multiple paid holidays and ample sick leave. Why didn't I have that? Because I settled for less than what I deserved, both in my jobs and my relationships. My boss got angry if I missed a day and gave me the silent treatment and a guilt trip as benefits. I took what came along instead of pursuing a career path with a viable future, asking for what I wanted.

Added to my list of must-haves was an emotionally healthy and professionally mature leader. One that I could respect, learn from, and aspire to be. Now that excited me! How to get there? Insurance kept rising to the top of the search list. PTSD (Post Traumatic Stress Disorder) left over from Blue Cross Blue Shield kept me from considering that path. I associated insurance with my nervous breakdown. In my mind, insurance was a causality for my demise, and I never wanted to go there again. I mentioned to Brian the top jobs seemed to be in insurance, but I was afraid. As soon as he heard the words insurance, he responded with positivity.

Brian knows stuff. More than intelligence, its wisdom combined with intuition. Akin to mind-reading, fortune-telling, or foreseeing. I don't know what you call it, but he's rarely wrong. I'd told him of jobs I was interested in or about offers from several companies. Every time, he advised me to pass. He said he felt something good was coming my way and that I should hold out. So, I waited.

But he jumped all over the insurance idea. Told me he'd help me study to get my license, pay for my books, and support me in any way he could. That was a sign. I researched the industry, scoured job sites, and read up on requirements. Medicare seemed a viable solution. I belong to the tail-end of the baby boomers, the last year born that is part of the boomer generation. There were millions ahead of me retiring or soon to retire. Remote Medicare jobs were prolific. Covid forced many insurance companies to be remote. They had to allow people to work from home to keep a workforce. Some companies help you get your health and accident license, but most require you to have the license to apply. One thing that was overwhelming for me in insurance was all the products and the knowledge it requires to be proficient. I remember steering clear of Medicare sales during open enrollment, passing them to my assistant because it was so complicated. There was so much to know, and it stressed me out.

Why not focus on Medicare?

Pick one area of insurance and become an expert instead of trying to learn a plethora of products. After checking out New Mexico's rules, licensing fees, and required tests, I confirmed with Brian that it was a wonderful decision to pursue my life, health, and accident license. Medicare only required health and accident licenses, but I might as well get all three. The test for three licenses added another 50 questions to the test. I could handle that, right?

Not convinced I could do it, Brian had to push me along. He ordered my books, spent hours putting together test questions into an easy-to-read document, and encouraged me to jump in. It took lunch hours in my car pouring over the material, weekends spent reading, and trial tests to determine when I was ready to take the big test. I was older this time, had a harder time recalling what I read, not sure I could pass the 150 questions.

Jinx was with me. He believed in me and let me know by laying on an open book left on the floor, jumping in my lap for attention after hours of study, lounging along the armrest of my chair, and purring encouragement. Finally, Brian said, "Take the test; you're ready." I didn't feel ready as I scheduled an online exam for the following weekend.

I had to take off all my rings and clear the room, leaving only the desk with nothing but my computer and a pencil. Two and a half hours. 150 questions. A stranger peering at me from my laptop camera made me more than nervous. I was a wreck. The first 20 questions were so hard I was sure I'd ordered the wrong test.

I'm so screwed.

I can't remember this.

I didn't study hard enough.

My old thought patterns came back.

I heard Mr. Jinx. from the other side of a closed door. He poked a paw under the small space between the door and the carpet and made me laugh. That was a sign.

I can do this.

I know this stuff.

I'm going to pass this test.

Sweat on my forehead, hands shaking as the timer clicked away, counting down the minutes. Fifty questions to go.

When I closed the computer and said goodbye to the stranger, I almost collapsed. I hate tests.

"I think I passed," I said when Brian asked. "But barely. It was much harder than I remembered."

"I know you passed," Brian said. "I predict you got a 76%."

Less than an hour later, I got an email saying they had posted my test results.

Shit. I was afraid to look.

Brian's words echoed in my mind.

"All you need to pass is a 70%."

Right. A 70% that's all I need.

I had to look three times and re-read the score. I blew it up on my screen, so I wasn't mistaken.

Congratulations! You passed with a 96%.

Tears of joy streamed down my face. I did more than pass. I kicked that test's ass!

A higher score than I received when I was 12 years younger. Who passes with 96%?

Me.

I did.

I can do this. I am smart. Smarter than I think I am.

About time I believed it.

My future changed that day. All the hardships, poor decisions, and tough situations leading up to that moment brought me to this place of happiness.

I worked hard, set a clear picture of what I wanted, and went after it. This time, I didn't sit back and let it happen. I made it happen. It took me 55 years to learn what some people do in their teens or twenties: how to take initiative. The best defense is a good offense. I know that's the opposite of what they say in football. But that was my lesson. I spent far too long not knowing what I wanted, settling for less than the best, reacting to my poor decisions, then wallowing in self-pity and blaming everyone else for the sorry state of my life.

The good thing about learning the hard way? The lesson remains. It's so painful, but when you finally learn the lesson, you remember. When you catch yourself about to make that mistake again, the pain comes back. Do this, and that will happen. Don't do that, and this will happen. I think it's called *experience*. Once you learn a lesson, you get to teach others. I believe that's called *wisdom*.

I pray for wisdom every day. Not riches, fame, or power. Wisdom.

Happiness follows wisdom. Ever notice how some older folks' glow with happiness? Love spills out of their lives, shines in their eyes, and flows in their veins. They have seen hard times, known genuine pain, and lived through hell and back. Yet, they are happy. Why? Because they learned their lessons, lived to talk about it, and discovered love is the answer. That is happiness. Genuine happiness. Love conquers all. When your heart is so full, it spills over to everyone and everything. That is the secret to life that a select few learn.

I have entered this season of life. I am grateful for every tear shed, every bump along the way, and every broken heart. Without the hard times, you cannot fully appreciate the good times. Gratitude and love are the greatest gifts. When those two things fill your heart, soul, and mind, happiness will follow. Not just gratitude for good things or happy times but gratitude for everything. When you learn gratitude, you will find something good in every situation.

We were together for about a year before the first episode hit. Brian was with Mulan as she seized, thrashing, in her crate. Yellow saliva oozed from her mouth. He told me about it, saying maybe it was an isolated incident.

Until it happened again, the episodes were rare at first, spaced weeks apart. They became more frequent and violent. We tried various food, supplements, and remedies before resorting to drugs. I could have dealt with the seizures, hard as they were to watch. But then, the rash showed up on her face. It started around her eyes, spread down to her nose, almost covering her face. We thought it was some kind of fungus. We took her to the vet, got an ointment, and waited. It got worse. Then her underbelly turned dark and purplish blue in large areas.

Back to the vet. Each time Brian accompanied us, picking up the bill. We weren't living together. I had my house; he had his. He didn't have to help. I never asked. He just stepped up, insisting on paying the bill.

We went out often. He showered me and my pets with love and affection, freely given, without asking for anything in return. If I was sick, he ran to the store, brought me food, walked the dog, fed the cat, and coddled me.

Brian was with me the day we got the news about Mulan. She had an incurable auto-immune disease that would progress, require lifelong treatment with expensive drugs, and she would suffer a great deal. That, combined with the seizures, led me to the decision to end her pain. Brian supported me either way. He let me decide.

We sat in the vet's office, Brian holding Mulan, comforting her. Me holding back tears. When she passed, he was there as I wept. He never shed a tear. I realized it wasn't because he didn't hurt; he stayed strong for me. I needed his strength. To let someone else carry the burden for once. I had shouldered enough.

A few days later, we took off work and went for a hike, Mulan's collar with us. We went to her favorite trail, said our goodbyes, and left the blue collar hanging from a tree. That's the way I wanted it. What a stark contrast to the last time I had to do this. I had found a good man at last. And we still had Mr. Jinx. I was grateful for that.

Lesson number ten learned: Two is better than one.

LESSON #11:
CATS ARE SMARTER THAN PEOPLE

It had been eight years since I left Wyoming. I'd had 11 different roommates, moved 6 times, dated countless men, and tried various jobs. Friends came and went, but the one constant in my life was Mr. Jinx. He'd been there through it all. When you go through so much change, it is comforting to have one constant in your life.

I overlook his bad habits, like throwing up fur balls the size of small rodents, dragging in debris, and leaving hair on the furniture. When I get frustrated after stepping barefoot in yet another wet pile of vomit, I remind myself that we are friends. It means he came home alive yet again, so instead of being angry, I smile. He is a pain, but he is my pain, and I love him.

Sometimes Mr. Jinx will come and sit close, just to be near me. Lying at my feet while I'm doing dishes or fixing my hair in the mirror is a favorite pastime for him. Pawing under a closed door if I'm on the other side as if to say, "I know you're in there. I want to be where you are." Maybe cats don't feel love like we do, but they form a strong bond with their owners.

Mr. Jinx is also smart. I knew he was intelligent, but one day he showed me just how smart he was.

Remember my roommate Janella? The one that moved to New York to seek her fortune? Our paths would cross again. When we lived in Flagstaff, she would visit family members in Albuquerque. She often invited me to join her, which I politely declined. Albuquerque? Why would I want to go there? Janella told me many times she planned to move there and retire. That seemed a long way from upstate New York.

I thought I would stay in Arizona for the rest of my life. Albuquerque was not on my radar while we were roommates. It never crossed my mind that we would both live there one day. Life is funny like that. It has its own rules and ways to surprise us. We didn't talk very often, but each time we did, she would tell me of one more job she'd applied for in Albuquerque.

A couple of years later, Janella was sitting on my back porch. She took a job in Santa Fe, a mere 30 minutes away. We celebrated like old times, relaxing in my happy place. The wine and conversation flowed as we reminisced and made plans for fresh adventures. She always called Mr.

Jinx, Jinxy. They reunited, Jinxy soaking up the attention on her lap while we carried on.

When he had his fill, he moved to his favorite spot under the honeysuckle. A small opening, like a cave surrounded by bushes, provided shade. He napped while we partied. My chair was facing Jinxy and the yard, so I saw it first. A kangaroo mouse bounding across the yard. Boing! Boing! Boing! It bounced high and fast, crossing in front of Mr. Jinx, who was sound asleep.

Janella and I had a good laugh, watching the mouse cross the yard, then scurry below a landscape timber. The rodent was mocking the cat, and we were making merry at the ironic situation. Poor kitty, right under his nose.

The bottle of wine was long empty, the sun was setting, and we were all talked out. Janella got up to leave when a very curious thing happened. Mr. Jinx approached with the mouse in his jaws, dropped it in front of us, then turned and walked away. The mouse was alive as it scurried for cover.

We stood there with our mouths open. The joke was on us. Mr. Jinx knew all along the mouse was there. He was the king of the castle. He decided who lived and who died. We were merely his mortal subjects.

Lesson number eleven learned: Cats are smarter than people.

Mr. Jinx and I have had many good years together. He continues to teach me life's most important lessons.

We're both living a happy, active life. I've been dating that good man for 4 years. Brian passed the Jinx test with flying colors. In fact, sometimes Jinx prefers his lap to mine. I have a job working remotely for a Medicare brokerage. After only one year as an agent, a start-up company hired me as a sales manager to handle a team and help them build from the ground up. My healing was complete. I was ready to manage again, able to handle the stress by staying in balance. The skills I learned along my path to happiness now serve me well.

I get to pour love on my team, leading them with wisdom and helping lift them up with encouragement. I know what it is to hit bottom and struggle with anxiety, depression, and hopelessness. Being able to relate with empathy and offer strength as they grow in their journey is priceless. Many bring their pain, brokenness, and inner struggles to work. I give them my best, from a full heart and life, for however long they are in my care. Striving to be the manager I wished I'd had. When I fail, I don't wallow; I learn and move on. My boss is an amazing leader. The company offers me more than enough time off. My pay is rewarding, and I love my job. Everything I envisioned and worked for came true. It took much longer and cost more than I imagined, but I wouldn't trade those years recovering for anything. It made me the woman I am today. Full of life, love, and gratitude.

I have a peaceful home, and I continue to find adventures. Someday, Mr. Jinx won't come home, or he'll fall asleep for good, but as of October 2022, he's still with me, so I focus on that. I hope to have another dog one day, maybe down the road when Jinx takes his last journey, but for now, Jinx and I are happy.

The lessons in this book changed my life, and I hope they help you. Sometimes I have to remind myself of a specific lesson to get back on track. It took me years to recover, much longer than I expected. Each step took me closer to happiness, even if it seemed like bad things kept happening. Deciding to be happy in spite of my circumstances, taking charge of my life, and accepting responsibility for my decisions changed my future. Before I began the long journey of healing, I allowed other people to steal my joy. Believing it was their fault that I was miserable. If only *they* would do this or stop doing that, I would be happy.

Learning to control my thoughts and changing how I reacted to a situation set me free. Allowing my inner child to have fun was a key point in my recovery. As I did, my creative side came alive. As creativity returned, I felt free. Having fun led to more happiness. I was lucky to discover my SAD (seasonal affective disorder) when I did, or I might have suffered much longer.

Being grateful for every little thing was the biggest lesson I learned. I call it my "attitude of gratitude."

Focusing on the good, instead of wallowing in the bad, empowers me every day, allowing me to live my best life. So many steps went into my recovery. It all started that day at the shelter, my daughter begging for a cat I didn't want. I will always be grateful for Mr. Jinx because… happiness came with a cat.

EPILOGUE

Life is funny. The longer I live, the more serendipitous it seems. I finished this manuscript and sent it to my editor, waiting to get his opinion. The same day I sent the manuscript, Brian proposed to me. I had been living with him for a few weeks while we worked on the floors of my house. Of course, Mr. Jinx came with me! But my plan was to return to my home as soon as we completed the flooring.

I was worried at first. Brian's neighborhood was full of cats. Were we going to relive the same nightmare, where my cat gets beat up all the time? I didn't mention my fear, but I worried prior to moving in. But Brian knew, he always knows. I swear that man can read my mind.

He brought up the subject first. I stated my fears about all the cats. How would Mr. Jinx survive? He's older now. There is only one of him and so many of them. There was one black and white feline I was especially worried about. He often came into the yard uninvited. He looked intimidating and mean.

Brian assured me he would handle the cat conundrum. He reasoned this would need to be addressed, and we might as well tackle it now. The situation between Adventure Man's house and Brian's house was a stark contrast. Brian built a fenced-in cat room off his back porch, open to the outside, furnished it with a tall cat tree, and had a cat box ready. Still, I was concerned about my cat's safety.

"We'll keep Mr. Jinx corralled for a couple of weeks. He can go outside and get used to things before he roams the neighborhood. He'll be fine," Brian assured me. How can you argue with someone that goes to such lengths to make sure your cat is comfortable and safe?

Exactly. You can't. So, I moved enough stuff to his house for a few weeks. But I wasn't moving in for good. I made that clear. Not going to play the long-term, live-in girlfriend game again. A few weeks turned into months and then he proposed.

My new life motto is, "Things take longer and cost more than you imagined." Remember that, and it won't surprise you when it happens. You can say, "Cynthia told me it would be like this." Smile.

It happened a few days after we allowed Mr. Jinx to be free. Brian made a cat-sized opening in the wire mesh enclosure so Jinx could wander in and out at leisure. I heard cat screams outside early one morning. I bolted outside to see not one but three feline bullies surrounding Mr. Jinx. The primary culprit was the black and white meanie, I suspected, about to pounce on my poor kitty.

I threw rocks and yelled at the cats, shooing them away. Mr. Jinx ran for cover just in time. Now I was afraid. The next night, the cats awoke Brian. Black and white was back with a vengeance on his mind, and Mr. Jinx was on his hit list. Not for long, mister. Brian was now part of Mr. Jinx's clowder and he was having none of this. The next day, a box with a slingshot and clay balls showed up. Enough to come close to the critter and scare him away, not enough to do any damage.

Funny, the black and white cat quit coming into our yard. Jinx wanders the neighborhood, but not too far from safety. His coat is shiny, his tail is full (he's not pulling the hair out), and he seems to smile often. He is welcome on the master bed (except at night), joins us on the couch whenever he wants, and enjoys the protection of a good man. We are all happy.

Lesson number twelve learned: Sometimes we all need a little help - even when you're a cat.

Want to read more of Cynthia Star's books? Check out my website at **CynthiaStarBooks.com** (click on Adult Genre for adult books). I have a dragon series that your kids might love!

ABOUT THE AUTHOR

When I was growing up, I read every dog or horse book I could get my hands on. I loved reading so much that I dreamed of being an author and wrote my first book at age 10. I was lucky enough to grow up on a farm in rural Nebraska, then spent 30 years in wonderful Wyoming before moving to the Southwest. I now live in Albuquerque, hiking the foothills often while I dream up my next story. This is my seventh book, and first book in an adult genre.

You can check out all my books at
www.CynthiaStarBooks.com
(know anyone who likes dragons?)

If this book helped you, I'd love to hear about it.
Email me at: CynaStar019@gmail.com.

Would you take the time to leave an honest review on Amazon? Reviews help readers find the right books, so thank you!

RECOMMENDED

Here are a few books that added to my healing, and I highly recommend them:

Transitions: Making Sense of Life's Changes by William Bridges

This book was monumental in helping me understand and deal with life's changes. Named one of the 50 all-time best books in self-help and personal development, I still revert to the lessons found in these pages.

Loving What Is: Four Questions That Can Change Your Life by Byron Katie

The four questions in this book, called The Work, changed my life and how I think about my problems. It enabled me to see what was troubling me in a different light. As Katie says, "It's not the problem that causes our suffering; it's our thinking about the problem."

Made in the USA
Monee, IL
24 June 2023